TOGAF™ VERSION 8.1.1 ENTERPRISE EDITION
A POCKET GUIDE

2008.

About the TOGAF series

The TOGAF series contains the official publications on TOGAF on behalf of The Open Group, including:

- TOGAF™ 2007 Edition (Incorporating 8.1.1)
- TOGAF™ Version 8.1.1 Enterprise Edition – Study Guide
- TOGAF™ Version 8.1.1 Enterprise Edition – A Pocket Guide

For the latest information on TOGAF, visit www.opengroup.org/togaf.

Other publications by Van Haren Publishing

Van Haren Publishing (VHP) specializes in titles on Best Practices, methods and standards within IT and business management.
These publications are grouped in the following series: *ITSM Library* (on behalf of ITSMF International), *Best Practice* and *IT Management Topics*.
VHP is also publisher on behalf of leading companies and institutions; e.g., The Open Group, IPMA-NL, CA, Getronics, Pink Elephant.

For the latest information on VHP publications, visit www.vanharen.net.

TOGAF™ Version 8.1.1 Enterprise Edition
A POCKET GUIDE

THE *Open* GROUP
www.opengroup.org

Van Haren
PUBLISHING

Title:	TOGAF™ Version 8.1.1 Enterprise Edition – A Pocket Guide
A Publication of:	The Open Group
Authors:	Terence Blevins, MITRE Corporation
	Professor Rachel Harrison, Stratton Edge Consulting
	Paul Homan, IBM
	Andrew Josey, The Open Group
	Matthew F. Rouse, EDS
	Tom van Sante, Getronics
Publisher:	Van Haren Publishing, Zaltbommel, www.vanharen.net
ISBN	978 90 8753 095 2
Edition:	1st edition, October 2007
Layout and Cover design:	CO2 Premedia, Amersfoort-NL
Print:	Wilco, Amersfoort-NL
Copyright:	© 2007, The Open Group

Contents

Preface

This Document

This Pocket Guide is based on TOGAF™ Version 8.1.1 Enterprise Edition. It is intended to help architects focus on the efficient and effective operations of their organization and senior managers understand the basics of The Open Group Architecture Framework (TOGAF). It is organized as follows:

- Chapter 1 provides a high-level view of TOGAF, enterprise architecture, and the contents of TOGAF.
- Chapter 2 provides an introduction to the Architecture Development Method (ADM), the method that TOGAF provides to develop enterprise architectures.
- Chapter 3 provides an overview of the key processes and deliverables of the ADM cycle.
- Chapter 4 provides an introduction to the Enterprise Continuum, a high-level concept that can be used with the ADM to develop an enterprise architecture.
- Chapter 5 provides an introduction to the TOGAF Resource Base, a set of resources, guidelines, processes, checklists, templates, and background information provided for architects to use during an application of the ADM.
- Appendix A provides a set of guidelines for developing a Business Scenario.
- Appendix B gives information on suggested further reading, including White Papers and example Business Scenarios.

The audience for this document is:

- Enterprise architects, business architects, IT architects, data architects, systems architects, solutions architects, and senior managers seeking a first introduction to TOGAF

A prior knowledge of IT architecture is not required. After reading this document, the reader seeking further information should refer to the TOGAF 8.1.1 Enterprise Edition documentation[1] available online.

Conventions Used in this Document

The following conventions are used throughout this document in order to help identify important information and avoid confusion over the intended meaning:

- Ellipsis (…)

  Indicates a continuation; such as an incomplete list of example items, or a continuation from preceding text.

- **Bold**

  Used to highlight specific terms.

- *Italics*

  Used for emphasis. May also refer to other external documents.

About The Open Group

The Open Group is a vendor-neutral and technology-neutral consortium, whose vision of Boundaryless Information Flow™ will enable access to integrated information within and between enterprises based on open standards and global interoperability. The Open Group works with customers, suppliers, consortia, and other standards bodies. Its role is to capture, understand, and address current and emerging requirements, establish policies, and share best practices; to facilitate interoperability, develop consensus, and evolve and integrate specifications and Open Source technologies; to offer a comprehensive set of services to enhance the operational efficiency of consortia; and to operate the industry's premier certification service.

---

1 The Open Group Architecture Framework (TOGAF), Version 8.1, Enterprise Edition, 2007 Edition incorporating TOGAF 8.1.1 (ISBN: 9789087530945), available at the bookshop at www.vanharen.net

Further information on The Open Group is available at
www.opengroup.org.

The Open Group has over 15 years' experience in developing and
operating certification programs and has extensive experience developing
and facilitating industry adoption of test suites used to validate
conformance to an open standard or specification.

The Open Group publishes a wide range of technical documentation, the
main part of which is focused on development of Technical and Product
Standards and Guides, but which also includes White Papers, Technical
Studies, and Business Titles.

A catalog is available at www.opengroup.org/bookstore.

About the Authors

Terence Blevins, MITRE Corporation

Terence Blevins is a MITRE employee supporting the Air Force as Lead Architect, Air Force Agile Combat Support Architecture. Terry has been involved with the architecture discipline since the 1980s when he was at the NCR Corporation as Director of Strategic Architecture. He has been involved with evolving this discipline since 1996 when he first was introduced to The Open Group Architecture Forum. He was co-chair of the Architecture Forum and frequent contributor of content to TOGAF, including the Business Scenario Method. Terry was Vice President and CIO of The Open Group where he contributed to The Open Group Vision of Boundaryless Information Flow. Mr. Blevins holds undergraduate and Masters degrees in Mathematics from Youngstown State University. He is TOGAF 8 certified.

Professor Rachel Harrison, Stratton Edge Consulting

Rachel Harrison is a Visiting Professor of Computer Science at the University of Reading and Director of Stratton Edge Consulting. Formerly she was Professor of Computer Science, Head of the Department of Computer Science, and Director of Research for the School of System Engineering at the University of Reading. She obtained an MA in Mathematics from Oxford University, an MSc in Computer Science from UCL, and a PhD in Computer Science from the University of Southampton. Current research interests include enterprise architecture, systems' evolution, software metrics, requirements engineering, and process modeling. Her consultancy services include preparation of the TOGAF Study Guide and its accompanying training course materials for The Open Group. Professor Harrison is a member of the IEEE Computer Society, the ACM, the BCS, and is also a Chartered Engineer.

Paul Homan, IBM

Paul Homan is a Technology Strategy Consultant within IBM's Global Business Services. He is an Enterprise Architect with 20 years' experience in IT and highly passionate and practically experienced in Architecture, Strategy, Design Authority, and Governance areas. Paul is particularly interested in EA Leadership, Requirements Management, and Business Architecture. He joined IBM from end-user environments, having worked as Chief Architect in both the UK Post Office and Royal Mail. He has not only established EA practices, but has also lived with the results!

Andrew Josey, The Open Group

Andrew Josey is Director of Standards and Certification within The Open Group. He has led the development and operation of many of The Open Group's certification development projects, including industry-wide certification programs for the UNIX system, the Linux Standard Base, Schools Interoperability Framework, The Open Group Architecture Framework, The Open Group Certified IT Architect program, IEEE POSIX, S/MIME Secure Messaging, and Secure MIME Gateway. He is currently managing the standards development process for TOGAF.

Matthew F. Rouse, EDS

Matthew Rouse is a member of the EDS Global Architecture Capability. Matthew has 19 years' IS/IT experience in applications development, system architecture, IS/IT strategy, and enterprise architecture. He brings expertise in strategic IS/IT planning and architecture to ensure that enterprises align their IS/IT investments with their business objectives. Matthew is a Chartered IT Professional member of the British Computer Society, a Master Certified IT Architect, and a member of the IEEE Computer Society.

Tom van Sante, Getronics

Tom van Sante is Principal Consultant for Getronics. He started his career in IT over 25 years ago after studying architecture at the Technical University in Delft. Working in a variety of functions, from operations to management, he has always operated on the borders between business and IT. He was involved in the introduction and development of ITIL/ASL/BiSL in the Netherlands. Tom van Sante has worked in numerous appointments for the EU and Dutch ministries advising on the use of IT in modern society. He is currently responsible for the introduction and development of TOGAF within Getronics.

Acknowledgements

The Open Group gratefully acknowledges the following:

- Past and present members of The Open Group Architecture Forum for developing The Open Group Architecture Framework (TOGAF)
- Capgemini and SAP for contributed materials
- The following reviewers of this document:
  - Allen Brown
  - Geoff Burke
  - Per Foldager
  - Ed Harrington
  - Kevin Hyman
  - Judith Jones
  - Peter Oldershaw
  - Richard Schaeren
  - John Spencer
  - Serge Thorn
  - Simon Townson

Chapter 1
Introduction to TOGAF™

This chapter provides an introduction to TOGAF 8.1.1.

Topics addressed in this chapter include:

- TOGAF, its structure and content
- The kinds of architecture that TOGAF addresses

1.1   Introduction to TOGAF 8.1.1

TOGAF is an architecture framework – **The Open Group Architecture Framework**. Put simply, TOGAF is a tool for assisting in the acceptance, production, use, and maintenance of architectures. It is based on an iterative process model supported by best practices and a re-usable set of existing architectural assets.

TOGAF is developed and maintained by The Open Group Architecture Forum. The first version of TOGAF, developed in 1995, was based on the US Department of Defense Technical Architecture Framework for Information Management (TAFIM). Starting from this sound foundation, The Open Group Architecture Forum has developed successive versions of TOGAF at regular intervals and published each one on The Open Group public web site.

This document covers TOGAF 8.1.1. TOGAF 8.1 was first published in December 2003, with a minor revision in 2006 to address known defects and terminology inconsistencies, known as TOGAF 8.1.1.

TOGAF 8.1.1 can be used for developing a broad range of different IT architectures. TOGAF complements, and can be used in conjunction with, other frameworks that are more focused on specific deliverables for particular vertical sectors such as Government, Defense, and Finance. The

key to TOGAF is the method – the TOGAF Architecture Development
Method (ADM) – for developing an IT architecture that addresses business
needs.

1.2   Structure of the TOGAF Document

TOGAF is structured into four parts as summarized in Table 1.1.

Table 1.1 Structure of the TOGAF Document

Part I: Introduction	This part provides a high-level introduction to some of the key concepts behind enterprise architecture and in particular the TOGAF approach.
Part II: Architecture Development Method	This is the core of TOGAF. It describes the TOGAF Architecture Development Method (ADM) – a step-by-step approach to develop and use an enterprise architecture.
Part III: Enterprise Continuum	This part describes the TOGAF Enterprise Continuum, a virtual repository of architecture assets, which includes the TOGAF Foundation Architecture, and the Integrated Information Infrastructure Reference Model (III-RM).
Part IV: Resources	This part comprises the TOGAF Resource Base – a set of tools and techniques available for use in applying TOGAF and the TOGAF ADM.

1.3   What is Architecture in the Context of TOGAF?

ANSI/IEEE Std 1471-2000 defines "architecture" as:
*"The fundamental organization of a system, embodied in its components, their
relationships to each other and the environment, and the principles governing
its design and evolution."*

TOGAF embraces and extends this definition. In TOGAF, "architecture"
has two meanings depending upon the context:
- A formal description of a system, or a detailed plan of the system at a
  component level to guide its implementation

- The structure of components, their inter-relationships, and the principles and guidelines governing their design and evolution over time

1.4   What kinds of Architecture does TOGAF deal with?

TOGAF 8.1.1 covers the development of four related types of architecture. These four types of architecture are commonly accepted as subsets of an overall enterprise architecture, all of which TOGAF is designed to support. They are shown as follows in Table 1.2.

Table 1.2 Architecture Types Supported by TOGAF

Architecture Type	Description
Business (or Business Process) Architecture	The business strategy, governance, organization, and key business processes.
Data Architecture[2]	The structure of an organization's logical and physical data assets and data management resources.
Applications Architecture	A blueprint for the individual application systems to be deployed, their interactions, and their relationships to the core business processes of the organization.
Technology Architecture	The logical software and hardware capabilities that are required to support the deployment of business, data, and application services. This includes IT infrastructure, middleware, networks, communications, processing, and standards.

---

2 Data Architecture may sometimes be called Information Architecture in some organizations.

1.5   What does TOGAF Contain?

TOGAF is organized into three sections as illustrated in Figure 1.1, all of which provide some guidance on what the outputs of a TOGAF-derived architecture should be and how they should be structured:

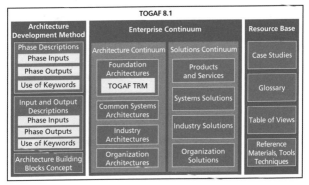

Figure 1.1 TOGAF Content Overview

The TOGAF concepts of Architecture Development Method, Enterprise Continuum, and Resource Base are intended to capture process, repository structure, and reference content respectively.

1.5.1 The TOGAF Architecture Development Method (ADM)

The **Architecture Development Method** (ADM) explains how to derive an organization-specific enterprise architecture that addresses business requirements. The TOGAF Architecture Development Method (ADM) is the major component of TOGAF and provides guidance for architects on a number of levels:

- It provides a number of **architecture development phases** (e.g., Business Architecture, Information Systems Architectures, Technology

Architecture) in a cycle, as an overall process template for architecture development activity.

- It provides a **narrative of each architecture phase**, describing the phase in terms of objectives, approach, inputs, steps, and outputs. The inputs and outputs sections provide an informal definition of the architecture content structure and deliverables.
- It provides cross-phase summaries covering requirements management, phase input, and phase output descriptions.

The ADM is described further in Chapter 2.

1.5.2 The Enterprise Continuum

The **Enterprise Continuum** provides a model for structuring an architecture repository – a "virtual repository" of all the architecture assets. This is based on architectures and solutions (models, patterns, architecture descriptions, etc.) that exist both within the enterprise and in the IT industry at large, and which the enterprise has collected for use in the development of architectures. Architecture Building Blocks reside within the Enterprise Continuum. At relevant places throughout the TOGAF ADM, there are reminders to consider which architecture assets the architect should use.

TOGAF itself provides two reference models for possible inclusion in an enterprise's own Enterprise Continuum.

The Enterprise Continuum is described further in Chapter 4.

1.5.3 The TOGAF Resource Base

The TOGAF **Resource Base**, "the reference content", is a set of resources, guidelines, templates, background information, etc. provided to be of assistance to the architect in the use of the ADM.

The TOGAF Resource Base is described further in Chapter 5.

Chapter 2
The Architecture
Development Method

This chapter describes the Architecture Development Method (ADM), its relationship to the rest of TOGAF, and high-level considerations for its use. It also includes a summary of each phase within the ADM.

Topics addressed in this chapter include:

- The TOGAF ADM and its relationship to other parts of TOGAF
- The phases of the TOGAF ADM
- The objectives, steps, inputs, and outputs to the ADM phases
- Requirements Management during the ADM cycle
- Scoping the Architecture Activity and adapting the ADM

2.1 What is the TOGAF ADM?

The Architecture Development Method (ADM), which forms the core of TOGAF, is a method for deriving organization-specific enterprise architectures and is the result of contributions from many architecture practitioners. It is specifically designed to address business requirements. The ADM describes:

- A reliable, proven way of developing and using an enterprise architecture
- A method of developing architectures on different levels[3] (business, applications, data, technology) that enable the architect to ensure that a complex set of requirements are adequately addressed
- Linkages to practical case studies
- Guidelines on tools for architecture development

---

3 In TOGAF this is termed as a set of architecture views.

2.2 What is its Relationship to Other Parts of TOGAF?

There are two other main parts to TOGAF, besides the ADM: the Enterprise Continuum (see Chapter 4) and the TOGAF Resource Base (see Chapter 5); these are used to support application of the ADM within an enterprise architecture project.

2.3 What are the Phases of the ADM?

The ADM consists of a number of phases that cycle through a range of architecture views that enable the architect to ensure that a complex set of requirements are adequately addressed. The basic structure of the ADM is shown in Figure 2.1.

The application of the ADM is an iterative process, over the whole process, between phases, and within phases. Throughout the ADM cycle, there should be frequent validation of results against the original expectations, both those for the whole ADM cycle, and those for the particular phase of the process. Such validation should reconsider scope, detail, schedules, and milestones. Each phase should consider assets produced from previous iterations of the process and external assets from the marketplace, such as other frameworks or models.

The ADM supports the concept of iteration at three levels:
- **Cycling around the ADM.** The ADM is presented in a circular manner indicating that the completion of one phase of architecture work directly feeds into subsequent phases of architecture work.
- **Iterating between phases.** TOGAF describes the concept of iterating across phases (e.g., returning to Business Architecture on completion of Technology Architecture).
- **Cycling around a single phase.** TOGAF supports repeated execution of the activities within a single TOGAF phase as a technique for elaborating architectural content.

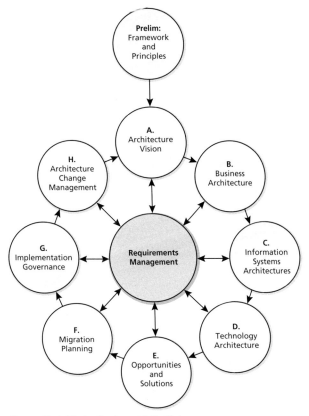

Figure 2.1 The Architecture Development Method Cycle

Table 2.1 Architecture Development Method Activities by Phase

ADM Phase	Activity
Preliminary Phase: Framework & Principles	Prepare the organization for successful TOGAF architecture projects.
Requirements Management	Every stage of a TOGAF project should be based on and validate business requirements. Requirements are identified, stored, and fed in and out of the relevant ADM phases, which dispose of, address, and prioritize requirements.
Phase A: Architecture Vision	Set the scope, constraints, and expectations for a TOGAF project. Validate the business context and create the Statement of Architecture Work.
Phase B: Business Architecture Phase C: Information Systems Architectures (Applications & Data) Phase D: Technology Architecture	Develop architectures at three levels: 1. Business 2. Information Systems 3. Technology In each case develop the Baseline ("as is") and Target ("to be") Architecture and analyze gaps.
Phase E: Opportunities & Solutions	Identify major implementation projects.
Phase F: Migration Planning	Analyze cost benefits and risk. Produce implementation roadmap.
Phase G: Implementation Governance	Architecture Contracts are prepared and issued by the Implementation Governance Board to ensure that the implementation project conforms to the architecture.
Phase H: Architecture Change Management	Ensure that the architecture responds to the needs of the enterprise.

2.4   The ADM in Detail

The following tables summarize the objectives, steps, and the inputs and outputs[4] of each phase of the ADM cycle.

2.4.1 Preliminary Phase: Framework & Principles

The Preliminary Phase prepares an organization to undertake successful enterprise architecture projects by defining how the organization is going to "do architecture".

An overview of the phase is given below:

Objectives	Steps
To confirm the commitment of the stakeholders	TOGAF does not define specific steps for this phase, suggesting that this phase adapt the ADM and that the two main aspects to this should be as follows: Defining "How we do Architecture": Principles and Frameworks Establishing IT Architecture Governance
To define the constraining principles	
To identify an organization's "architecture footprint"; that is, the people responsible for performing the architecture work, where they are located, and their responsibilities	
To define the scope and assumptions; this is particularly important for large organizations where there may be a federated architecture environment	
To define the framework and detailed methodologies that are going to be used to develop the enterprise architecture in the organization; this is typically an adaptation of the ADM	
To set up and monitor the framework's fitness-for-purpose; normally this includes an initial pilot project to check the viability of the approach within the organization	
To define the evaluation criteria for tools, repositories, and management processes to: capture, publish, and maintain architecture artifacts	

4 Version numbers for specific deliverables have been omitted from this Pocket Guide since TOGAF states that the ADM numbering scheme is an example and that it should be adapted as appropriate.

Inputs	Outputs
TOGAF Architecture Development Method (ADM)	Architecture principles
	Framework definition
Other architecture framework(s)	Restatement of business
Business strategy (including goals and drivers)	principles, goals, and drivers
IT governance strategy	
Architecture principles, including business principles	
Other federated architectures principles	

2.4.2 Phase A: Architecture Vision

Phase A is about project establishment and initiates an iteration of the architecture process, setting the scope, constraints and expectations for the iteration. It is required in order to validate the business context and to create the Statement of Architecture Work.

Objectives	Steps
Obtain management commitment for this particular cycle of the ADM	Project Establishment
	Identify Business Goals and Business Drivers
Validate business principles, goals, and drivers	Review Architecture Principles, including Business Principles
Define, scope, and prioritize architecture tasks	Define the scope
Identify stakeholders, their concerns, and objectives	Define Constraints
	Identify Stakeholders and Concerns, Business Requirements, and Architecture Vision
Define business requirements and constraints	
Describe appropriate solutions	Document the Statement of Architecture Work and Gain Approval
Obtain formal approval to proceed	
Understand the influence on, and from, parallel architecture developments	

Inputs	Outputs
Request for Architecture Work	Approved Statement of Architecture Work
Business strategy, business goals, and business drivers	Refined statements of business goals and strategic drivers
Architecture principles, including business principles	Architecture principles, including business principles
Enterprise Continuum; that is, existing architecture documentation (framework description, architecture descriptions, existing baseline descriptions, etc.)	Architecture Vision including:
	Baseline Business Architecture
	Baseline Data Architecture
	Baseline Applications Architecture
	Baseline Technology Architecture
	Target Business Architecture
	Target Data Architecture
	Target Applications Architecture
	Target Technology Architecture

2.4.3 Phase B: Business Architecture

Phase B is about documenting the fundamental organization of the business, embodied in its business processes and people, their relationships to each other and the environment, and the principles governing its evolution and design.

Objectives	Steps
Select architecture viewpoints to demonstrate how stakeholder concerns are addressed in the Business Architecture	Develop Baseline Business Architecture Description
	Identify Reference Models, Viewpoints, and Tools
Select tools and techniques for viewpoints	Create Business Architecture Model(s)
	Select Business Architecture Building Blocks
Describe the existing Business Architecture (the current baseline)	Conduct a Formal Checkpoint Review of the Architecture Model and Building Blocks with Stakeholders
Develop a Target Business Architecture	
Analyze the gaps between the Baseline and Target Architectures	Review Non-Functional (Qualitative) Criteria
	Complete the Business Architecture
	Perform Gap Analysis and Create Report

Inputs	Outputs
Request for Architecture Work	Statement of Architecture Work, updated if necessary
Approved Statement of Architecture Work	Validated business principles, business goals, and strategic drivers
Refined statements of business goals and strategic drivers	Baseline Business Architecture (detailed)
Architecture principles, including business principles	Target Business Architecture (detailed)
Enterprise Continuum	Views corresponding to the selected viewpoints addressing key stakeholder concerns
Architecture Vision, including:	Gap Analysis results
Baseline Business Architecture	Technical Requirements
Baseline Data Architecture	Business Architecture Report
Baseline Applications Architecture	Updated business requirements
Baseline Technology Architecture	
Target Business Architecture	
Target Data Architecture	
Target Applications Architecture	
Target Technology Architecture	

2.4.4 Phase C: Information Systems Architecture

Phase C is about documenting the fundamental organization of an organization's IT systems, embodied in the major types of information and the application systems that process them. There are two steps in this phase, which may be developed either in order or in parallel:

- Data Architecture
- Applications Architecture

2.4.4.1 Data Architecture

Objectives	Steps
Define the types and sources of data needed to support the business, in a way that can be understood by the stakeholders	Develop Baseline Architecture Description Review and Select Principles, Reference Models, Viewpoints, and Tools Create Data Architecture Model(s) Select Data Architecture Building Blocks Conduct a Checkpoint Review of the Architecture Model Review Qualitative Criteria Complete the Data Architecture Conduct Checkpoint/Impact Analysis Perform Gap Analysis and Create Report
Inputs	**Outputs**
Data principles Request for Architecture Work Statement of Architecture Work Architecture Vision Baseline Business Architecture Target Business Architecture Baseline Data Architecture Target Data Architecture Relevant Technical Requirements Gap Analysis results Re-usable building blocks (from organization's Enterprise Continuum)	Statement of Architecture Work Baseline Data Architecture Validated data principles, or new data principles Target Data Architecture Data Architecture views corresponding to the selected viewpoints Data Architecture Report Gap Analysis results Relevant Technical Requirements that will apply to this evolution of the architecture development cycle Impact Analysis Updated business requirements

2.4.4.2 Applications Architecture

Objectives	Steps
Define the kinds of application systems necessary to process the data and support the business	Develop Baseline Applications Architecture Description Review and Validate Principles, select Reference Models, Viewpoints, and Tools Create Architecture Models for each Viewpoint Identify Candidate Applications Conduct a Checkpoint Review Review the Qualitative Criteria Complete the Applications Architecture Perform Gap Analysis and Create Report
Inputs	**Outputs**
Application principles Request for Architecture Work Statement of Architecture Work Architecture Vision Relevant Technical Requirements Gap Analysis results (from Phase B: Business Architecture) Baseline Business Architecture Target Business Architecture Baseline Applications Architecture Target Applications Architecture Re-usable building blocks (from organization's Enterprise Continuum)	Statement of Architecture Work Baseline Applications Architecture Target Applications Architecture Validated application principles, or new application principles Applications Architecture views corresponding to the selected viewpoints Applications Architecture Report Gap Analysis results Impact Analysis Updated business requirements

2.4.5 Phase D: Technology Architecture

Phase D is about documenting the fundamental organization of the IT systems, embodied in the hardware, software and communications technology.

Objectives	Steps
To develop a Target Technology Architecture that will form the basis of the following implementation work	Develop Baseline Technology Architecture Description *Create Target Technology Architecture*: Create a Baseline Technology Architecture Description in services terminology Consider different Architecture Reference Models, Viewpoints, and Tools Create an Architecture Model of Building Blocks Select the Services Portfolio per Building Block Confirm that the Business Goals and Objectives are met Choose the Criteria for Specification Selection Complete the Architecture Definition Conduct Gap Analysis

Inputs	Outputs
Technology principles, if existing Request for Architecture Work Statement of Architecture Work Architecture Vision Baseline Business Architecture Baseline Data Architecture Baseline Applications Architecture Baseline Technology Architecture Target Business Architecture Target Data Architecture Target Applications Architecture Target Technology Architecture Relevant Technical Requirements Gap Analysis results (from Data Architecture and Applications Architecture) Re-usable building blocks	Statement of Architecture Work, updated if necessary Baseline Technology Architecture Validated technology principles or new technology principles (if generated here) Technology Architecture Report, summarizing what was done and the key findings Target Technology Architecture Technology Architecture, Gap Analysis report Viewpoints addressing key stakeholder concerns Views corresponding to the selected viewpoints

2.4.6 Phase E: Opportunities and Solutions

Phase E is the first phase which is directly concerned with implementation.
It identifies the parameters of change, the phases, and the necessary
projects using gap analysis on the business functions in the old
environment and the new.

Objectives	Steps
Evaluate and select implementation options (for example, build versus buy *versus* re-use) Identify the strategic parameters for change and the projects to be undertaken Assess the costs and benefits of the projects Generate an overall implementation and migration strategy and a detailed Implementation Plan	Identify the Key Business Drivers Review Gap Analysis from Phase D Brainstorm Technical Requirements Brainstorm Other Requirements Architecture Assessment and Gap Analysis Identify Work Packages or Projects
Inputs	**Outputs**
Request for Architecture Work Statement of Architecture Work Target Business Architecture Target Data Architecture Target Applications Architecture Target Technology Architecture Re-usable Architecture (Solution) Building Blocks from your organization's Enterprise Continuum Product information	Implementation and migration strategy High-level Implementation Plan Impact Analysis document – the project list section is documented in this phase

2.4.7 Phase F: Migration Planning

Phase F address migration planning; that is, how to move from the
Baseline to the Target Architectures.

Objectives	Steps
Sort the various implementation projects into priority Produce a prioritized list of projects that will form the basis of the detailed Implementation and Migration Plans	Prioritize Projects Estimate the resource requirements and available resources for each project Perform a cost/benefit analysis for each project to identify the projects that will make the most impact in proportion to their costs Perform a risk assessment for each project to identify any high risk projects Generate a proposed implementation roadmap Prepare a Migration Plan showing how existing systems will migrate to the new architecture

Inputs	Outputs
Request for Architecture Work Statement of Architecture Work Target Business Architecture Target Data Architecture Target Applications Architecture Target Technology Architecture Impact Analysis – project list	Impact Analysis – detailed Implementation Plan and Migration Plan (including Architecture Implementation Contract)

2.4.8 Phase G: Implementation Governance

Phase G defines the architecture constraints on the implementation projects and constructs and obtains signatures on an Architecture Contract. It also includes monitoring the implementation work.

Objectives	Steps
Formulate recommendations for each implementation project Construct an Architecture Contract to govern the overall implementation and deployment process Perform appropriate governance functions while the system is being implemented and deployed Ensure conformance with the defined architecture by implementation projects and other projects	Formulate Project Recommendations Document Architecture Contract Perform ongoing Implementation Governance
Inputs	**Outputs**
Request for Architecture Work Statement of Architecture Work Re-usable Solution Building Blocks (from the organization's Solutions Continuum) Impact Analysis – detailed Implementation Plan and Migration Plan (including Architecture Implementation Contract)	Impact Analysis – Implementation Recommendations Architecture Contract The architecture-compliant implemented system

2.4.9 Phase H: Architecture Change Management

Phase H ensures that changes to the architecture are managed in a controlled manner.

Objectives	Steps
Establish an architecture change management process Provide continual monitoring of changes in technology, business, etc. Determine whether to initiate a new architecture cycle or make changes to the framework and principles	Monitor Technology Changes Monitor Business Changes Assess Changes and Development of Position to Act Arrange Meeting of Architecture Board

Inputs	Outputs
Requests for Architecture Change due to technology changes Requests for Architecture Change due to business changes	Architecture updates Changes to architecture framework and principles New Request for Architecture Work, to initiate another cycle of the ADM

2.4.10   Requirements Management

The process of managing architecture requirements applies to all phases of the ADM cycle. The Requirements Management process is a dynamic process, which addresses the identification of requirements for the enterprise, storing them and then feeding them in and out of the relevant ADM phases. As shown in Figure 2.1, this process is central to driving the ADM process.

The ability to deal with changes in the requirements is crucial to the ADM process, since architecture by its very nature deals with uncertainty and change, bridging the divide between the aspirations of the stakeholders and what can be delivered as a practical solution.

Objectives	Steps
To provide a process to manage architecture requirements throughout the phases of the ADM cycle To identify requirements for the enterprise, store them and feed them in and out of the relevant ADM phases, which dispose of, address, and prioritize requirements	Identify/document requirements Baseline Requirements Monitor baseline requirements Identify changed requirement; remove, add, modify, and re-assess priorities Identify changed requirement and record priorities; identify and resolve conflicts; generate requirements impact statements Assess impact of changed requirement on current and previous ADM phases Implement requirements arising from Phase H Update the requirements repository Implement change in the current phase Assess and revise gap analysis for past phases

Inputs	Outputs
The inputs to the Requirements Management process are the requirements-related outputs from each ADM phase. The first high-level requirements are produced as part of the Architecture Vision. Each architecture domain then generates detailed requirements. Deliverables in later ADM phases contain mappings to new types of requirements (for example, conformance requirements).	Changed requirements Requirements Impact Statement, which identifies the phases of the ADM that need to be revisited to address any changes. The final version must include the full implications of the requirements (e.g., costs, timescales, and business metrics).

2.5 Scoping the Architecture Activity

The TOGAF ADM defines a recommended sequence for the various phases and steps involved in developing an organization-wide enterprise architecture, but the ADM cannot determine scope: this must be determined by the organization itself.

There are many reasons for wanting to limit the scope of the architecture activity to be undertaken, most of which come down to the availability of people, finance, and other resources. The scope chosen for the architecture activity is normally directly dependent on available resources, and, in the final analysis, is usually a question of feasibility.

Table 2.2 shows the four dimensions in which the scope may be defined and limited.

Table 2.2 Dimensions for Limiting the Scope of the Architecture Activity

Dimension	Considerations
Enterprise scope or focus	What is the full extent of the enterprise, and how much of that extent should the architecting effort focus on? Many enterprises are very large, effectively comprising a federation of organizational units that could validly be considered enterprises in their own right. The modern enterprise increasingly extends beyond its traditional boundaries, to embrace a fuzzy combination of traditional business enterprise combined with suppliers, customers, and partners.
Architecture domains	A complete enterprise architecture description should contain all four architecture domains (Business, Data, Applications, Technology), but the realities of resource and time constraints often mean there is not enough time, funding, or resources to build a top-down, all-inclusive architecture description encompassing all four architecture domains, even if the enterprise scope is chosen to be less than the full extent of the overall enterprise.
Vertical scope, or level of detail	To what level of detail should the architecting effort go? How much architecture is "enough"? What is the appropriate demarcation between the architecture effort and other, related activities (system design, system engineering, system development)?
Time horizon	What is the time horizon that needs to be articulated for the Architecture Vision, and does it make sense (in terms of practicality and resources) for the same horizon to be covered in the detailed architecture description? If not, how many intermediate Target Architectures are to be defined, and what are their time horizons?

2.6 Adapting the ADM

The ADM is a generic method for architecture development, which is designed to deal with most system and organizational requirements. However, it will often be necessary to modify or extend the ADM to suit specific needs. One of the tasks before applying the ADM is to review the process and its outputs for applicability, and then tailor them as appropriate to the circumstances of the individual enterprise. This activity may well produce an "enterprise-specific" ADM.

There are a number of reasons for wanting to tailor the ADM to the circumstances of an individual enterprise. Some of the reasons are outlined below:

1. An important consideration is that the order of the phases in the ADM is to some extent dependent on the maturity of the architecture discipline within the enterprise concerned. For example, if the business case for doing architecture is not well recognized, then creating an Architecture Vision is essential; and a detailed Business Architecture needs to come next to define the business case for the remaining architecture work, and secure the active participation of key stakeholders in that work.

2. The order of phases may also be defined by the business and architecture principles of an enterprise. For example, the business principles may dictate that the enterprise be prepared to adjust its business processes to meet the needs of a packaged solution, so that it can be implemented quickly to enable fast response to market changes. In such a case, the Business Architecture (or at least the completion of it) may well follow completion of the Information Systems Architecture.

3. An enterprise may wish to use or tailor the ADM in conjunction with another enterprise architecture framework that has a defined set of deliverables specific to a particular vertical sector: Government, Defense, e-Business, Telecommunications, etc.

4. The ADM is one of many corporate processes that make up the corporate governance model for an enterprise. The ADM is complementary to, and supportive of, other standard program management processes. The enterprise will tailor the ADM to reflect the relationships and dependencies with the other management processes.

5. The ADM is being mandated for use by a prime or lead contractor in an outsourcing situation, and needs to be tailored to achieve a suitable compromise between the contractor's existing practices and the contracting enterprise's requirements.

6. The enterprise is a small-to-medium enterprise, and wishes to use a "cut-down" version of the ADM that is more attuned to the reduced level of resources and system complexity typical of such an environment.

7. The enterprise is very large and complex, comprising many separate but interlinked "enterprises" within an overall collaborative business framework, and the architecture method needs to be adapted to recognize this. Such enterprises cannot usually be treated successfully as a single entity and a more federated approach is required.

Chapter 3
Key Processes and Deliverables of the ADM Cycle

This chapter will help you to understand the contents of key deliverables and processes of the ADM cycle. Table 3.1 gives a roadmap to this chapter by the ADM phase in which the deliverables and processes are used. For each point, key facts are presented.

Table 3.1 Roadmap to Chapter 3

ADM Phase	Reference(s)
Preliminary Phase: Framework & Principles	Section 3.1, Framework Definition
	Section 3.2, Architecture Principles
	Section 3.3, Business Principles, Goals, and Drivers
	Section 3.4, IT Governance Strategy
Phase A: Architecture Vision	Section 3.5, Request for Architecture Work
	Section 3.6, Statement of Architecture Work
	Section 3.7, Architecture Vision
	Section 3.20, Architecture Viewpoints
	Section 3.21, Architecture Views
Phase B: Business Architecture	Section 3.8, Business Architecture
	Section 3.9, Business Architecture Report
	Section 3.10, Business Requirements
	Section 3.11, Business Scenarios
	Section 3.12, Technical Requirements
	Section 3.13, Gap Analysis
	Section 3.20, Architecture Viewpoints
	Section 3.21, Architecture Views
	Section 3.22, Re-Usable Architecture Building Blocks
	Section 3.23, Re-Usable Solution Building Blocks

ADM Phase	Reference(s)
Phase C: Information Systems Architectures	Section 3.13, Gap Analysis Section 3.14, Data Architecture Section 3.15, Data Architecture Report Section 3.16, Applications Architecture Section 3.17, Applications Architecture Report Section 3.20, Architecture Viewpoints Section 3.21, Architecture Views Section 3.22, Re-Usable Architecture Building Blocks Section 3.23, Re-Usable Solution Building Blocks
Phase D: Technology Architecture	Section 3.13, Gap Analysis Section 3.18, Technology Architecture Section 3.19, Technology Architecture Report Section 3.20, Architecture Viewpoints Section 3.21, Architecture Views Section 3.22, Re-Usable Architecture Building Blocks Section 3.23, Re-Usable Solution Building Blocks
Phase E: Opportunities and Solutions	Section 3.22, Re-Usable Architecture Building Blocks Section 3.23, Re-Usable Solution Building Blocks Section 3.24, Impact Analysis Document – Project List Section 3.28, Product Information
Phase F: Migration Planning	Section 3.25, Impact Analysis Document – Migration Plan
Phase G: Implementation Governance	Section 3.26, Impact Analysis Document – Implementations Recommendations Section 3.27, Architecture Contracts
Phase H: Architecture Change Management	Section 3.29, Request for Architecture Changes Section 3.30, New Technology Reports Section 3.31, Requirements Impact Statement

3.1 Framework Definition

Selecting and defining a framework is the practical starting point for an architecture project. Building on TOGAF has a number of advantages over creating a framework from scratch:

- It avoids the initial panic when the scale of the task becomes apparent.
- Use of TOGAF is systematic – "codified common sense".

- TOGAF captures what others have found to work in real life.
- TOGAF has a baseline set of resources to re-use.
- TOGAF defines a Foundation Architecture in the Enterprise Continuum.

3.2   Architecture Principles

This set of documentation is an initial output of the Preliminary Phase. It is the set of general rules and guidelines for the architecture being developed. See TOGAF 8.1.1 Enterprise Edition Part IV: Resource Base, Architecture Principles for guidelines and a detailed set of generic architecture principles. The suggested contents of this document are business principles, data principles, applications principles, and technology principles.

3.2.1 Developing Architecture Principles

The Lead Architect, in conjunction with the enterprise CIO, Architecture Board, and other key business stakeholders, typically develops architecture principles.

The following typically influences the development of architecture principles:

- Enterprise mission and plans: the mission, plans, and organizational infrastructure of the enterprise.
- Enterprise strategic initiatives: the characteristics of the enterprise – its strengths, weaknesses, opportunities, and threats – and its current enterprise-wide initiatives (such as process improvement and quality management).
- External constraints: market factors (time-to-market imperatives, customer expectations, etc.); existing and potential legislation.
- Current systems and technology: the set of information resources deployed within the enterprise, including systems documentation, equipment inventories, network configuration diagrams, policies, and procedures.

- Computer industry trends: predictions about the usage, availability, and cost of computer and communication technologies, referenced from credible sources along with associated best practices presently in use.

3.2.2 Defining Architecture Principles

Depending on the organization, principles may be established at any or all of three levels:

- **Enterprise principles** provide a basis for decision-making and dictate how the organization fulfills its mission. Such principles are commonly found in governmental and not-for-profit organizations, but are also found in commercial organizations, as a means of harmonizing decision-making. They are a key element in a successful architecture governance strategy.
- **IT principles** provide guidance on the use and deployment of all IT resources and assets across the enterprise. They are developed to make the information environment as productive and cost-effective as possible.
- **Architecture principles** are a subset of IT principles that relate to architecture work. They reflect a level of consensus across the enterprise, and embody the spirit of the enterprise architecture. Architecture principles can be further divided into:
  - Principles that govern the architecture process, affecting the development, maintenance, and use of the enterprise architecture
  - Principles that govern the implementation of the architecture

TOGAF defines a standard way of describing principles. In addition to a definition statement, each principle should have associated rationale and implications statements, both to promote understanding and acceptance of the principles themselves, and to support the use of the principles in explaining and justifying why specific decisions are made.

Table 3.2 TOGAF Template for Defining Principles

Name	Should both represent the essence of the rule as well as be easy to remember. Specific technology platforms should not be mentioned in the name or statement of a principle. Avoid ambiguous words in the name and in the statement such as: "support", "open", "consider", and for lack of good measure the word "avoid", itself, be careful with "manage(ment)", and look for unnecessary adjectives and adverbs (fluff).
Statement	Should succinctly and unambiguously communicate the fundamental rule. For the most part, the principles statements for managing information are similar from one organization to the next. It is vital that the principles statement be unambiguous.
Rationale	Should highlight the business benefits of adhering to the principle, using business terminology. Point to the similarity of information and technology principles to the principles governing business operations. Also describe the relationship to other principles, and the intentions regarding a balanced interpretation. Describe situations where one principle would be given precedence or carry more weight than another for making a decision.
Implications	Should highlight the requirements, both for the business and IT, for carrying out the principle – in terms of resources, costs, and activities/tasks. It will often be apparent that current systems, standards, or practices would be incongruent with the principle upon adoption. The impact on the business and consequences of adopting a principle should be clearly stated. The reader should readily discern the answer to: "How does this affect me?" It is important not to oversimplify, trivialize, or judge the merit of the impact. Some of the implications will be identified as potential impacts only, and may be speculative rather than fully analyzed.

3.2.3 Qualities of Principles

There are five criteria that distinguish a good set of principles, as shown in Table 3.3.

Table 3.3 Recommended Criteria for Quality Principles

Criteria	Description
Understandability	The underlying tenets of a principle can be quickly grasped and understood by individuals throughout the organization. The intention of the principle is clear and unambiguous, so that violations, whether intentional or not, are minimized.
Robustness	Principles should enable good quality decisions about architectures and plans to be made, and enforceable policies and standards to be created. Each principle should be sufficiently definitive and precise to support consistent decision-making in complex, potentially controversial situations.
Completeness	Every potentially important principle governing the management of information and technology for the organization is defined. The principles cover every situation perceived.
Consistency	Strict adherence to one principle may require a loose interpretation of another principle. The set of principles must be expressed in a way that allows a balance of interpretations. Principles should not be contradictory to the point where adhering to one principle would violate the spirit of another. Every word in a principle statement should be carefully chosen to allow consistent yet flexible interpretation.
Stability	Principles should be enduring, yet able to accommodate changes. An amendment process should be established for adding, removing, or altering principles after they are ratified initially.

3.2.4 Applying Architecture Principles

Architecture principles are used to capture the fundamental truths about how the enterprise will use and deploy IT resources and assets. The principles are used in a number of different ways:

1. To provide a framework within which the enterprise can start to make conscious decisions about IT

2. As a guide to establishing relevant evaluation criteria, thus exerting strong influence on the selection of products or product architectures in the later stages of managing compliance to the IT architecture

3. As drivers for defining the functional requirements of the architecture

4. As an input to assessing both existing IS/IT systems and the future strategic portfolio, for compliance with the defined architectures; these assessments will provide valuable insights into the transition activities needed to implement an architecture, in support of business goals and priorities

5. The Rationale statements (see below) highlight the value of the architecture to the enterprise, and therefore provide a basis for justifying architecture activities

6. The Implications statements (see below) provide an outline of the key tasks, resources, and potential costs to the enterprise of following the principle; they also provide valuable inputs to future transition initiatives and planning activities

7. To support the architecture governance activities in terms of:
   – Providing a "back-stop" for the standard Architecture Compliance assessments where some interpretation is allowed or required
   – Supporting a decision to initiate a dispensation request where the implications of a particular architecture amendment cannot be resolved within local operating procedure

Principles are inter-related, and need to be applied as a set. Principles will sometimes compete; for example, the principles of "accessibility" and "security". Each principle must be considered in the context of "all other things being equal". At times a decision will be required as to which principle will take precedence on a particular issue. The rationale for such decisions should always be documented. The fact that a principle seems self-evident does not mean that the principle is actually observed in an organization, even when there are verbal acknowledgements of the principle. Although specific penalties are not prescribed in a declaration of principles, violations of principles generally cause operational problems and inhibit the ability of the organization to fulfill its mission.

3.3   Business Principles, Goals, and Drivers

A statement of the business principles, goals, and drivers has usually been defined elsewhere in the enterprise prior to the architecture activity. They are restated as an output of the Preliminary Phase and reviewed again as a part of Phase A: Architecture Vision. The activity in Phase A is to ensure that the current definitions are correct and clear. The TOGAF Resource Base (see Chapter 5) contains an example set of eight business principles that are a useful starting point.

3.4   IT Governance Strategy

An IT governance strategy, and an appropriate organization for implementing the strategy, must be established with the backing of top management, clarifying who owns the enterprise's IT resources, and, in particular, who has ultimate responsibility for their enterprise-wide integration. IT governance is a broad topic and outside of the scope of the TOGAF document. TOGAF recommends COBIT as a source for further information.

3.5   Request for Architecture Work

This is a document that is sent from the sponsoring organization to the architecture organization. Often it is produced with the assistance of the architecture organization. It is an input to Phase A: Architecture Vision. In general all the information in this document should be at a high level. The suggested contents of this document are as follows:

• Organization sponsors
• Organization's mission statement
• Business goals (and changes)

- Strategic plans of the business
- Time limits
- Changes in the business environment
- Organizational constraints
- Budget information, financial constraints
- External constraints, business constraints
- Current business system description
- Current architecture/IT system description
- Description of developing organization
- Description of resources available to developing organization

3.6   Statement of Architecture Work

The Statement of Architecture Work is created as a deliverable of Phase
A, and is effectively a contract between the architecting organization and
the sponsor of the architecture project. This document is a response to
the Request for Architecture Work input document (see Section 3.5). It
should describe an overall plan to address the request for work and propose
how solutions to the problems that have been identified will be addressed
through the architecture process. The suggested contents of this document
are as follows:

- Statement of work title
- Project request and background
- Project description and scope
- Architecture Vision
- Managerial approach
- Change of scope procedures
- Responsibilities and deliverables
- Acceptance criteria and procedures
- Project plan and schedule
- Support of the Enterprise Continuum (re-use)
- Signature approvals

3.7   Architecture Vision

A key step in Phase A is to identify key stakeholders and their concerns; define key business requirements and articulate an Architecture Vision to address them, within the scope and constraints, whilst conforming to business and architecture principles. Business scenarios are an appropriate and important technique that can be used as part of the process in developing an Architecture Vision document. Note that they can be used at various stages of the ADM. They are a method for ensuring that the enterprise architecture being produced is linked to business requirements. See Section 3.1 and Appendix A for more information. The suggested contents are as follows:

- Problem description:
  - Purpose of scenario
- Detailed objectives
- Environment and process models:
  - Process description
  - Process steps mapped to environment
  - Process steps mapped to people
  - Information flow
- Actors and their roles and responsibilities:
  - Human actors and roles
  - Computer actors and roles
  - Requirements
- Resulting architecture model:
  - Constraints
  - IT principles
  - Architecture supporting the process
  - Requirements mapped to architecture

3.8   Business Architecture

The objective of Phase B is to develop the Business Architecture. The topics that should be addressed in the Business Architecture are as follows:

- Baseline Business Architecture: this is a description of the existing Business Architecture
- Business goals, objectives, and constraints:
  - Business requirements and key system and architecture drivers
  - Business return given required changes
  - Assumptions (e.g., business, financial, organizational, or required technical functionality)
  - Business Architecture principles
- Business Architecture models:
  - Organization structure
  - Business functions
  - Business roles
  - Correlation of organization and functions
  - Business Architecture Building Blocks list (e.g., business services)
  - Business Architecture Building Blocks models
  - Candidate Solution Building Blocks list
  - Candidate Solution Building Blocks models
  - Relevant business process descriptions, including measures and deliverables
- Technical Requirements (drivers for other architecture work)

3.9   Business Architecture Report

The Business Architecture Report, produced in Phase B, is a log of the architecture activity undertaken in the phase, and rationale for any key decisions.

3.10 Business Requirements

The business scenarios technique is used to discover and document business requirements.

3.11 Business Scenarios

The ADM has its own method (a "method-within-a-method") for identifying and articulating the business requirements implied in new business functionality to address key business drivers, and the implied Technology Architecture requirements. This process is known as "business scenarios".

A business scenario is a description of a business problem, which enables requirements to be viewed in relation to one another in the context of the overall problem. Without such a description to serve as context, the business value of solving the problem is unclear, the relevance of potential solutions is unclear, and there is a danger of the solution being based on an inadequate set of requirements.

A key factor in the success of any other major project is the extent to which it is linked to business requirements, and demonstrably supports and enables the enterprise to achieve its business objectives. Business scenarios are an important technique to help identify and understand business needs. A set of guidelines for developing business scenarios is given in Appendix A.

The technique may be used iteratively, at different levels of detail in the hierarchical decomposition of the Business Architecture. The generic business scenario process is as follows:

- Identify, document, and rank the problem that is driving the project
- Document, as high-level architecture models, the business and technical environments where the problem situation is occurring
- Identify and document desired objectives; the results of handling the problems successfully
- Identify human actors and their place in the business model, the human participants, and their roles

- Identify computer actors and their place in the technology model, the computing elements, and their roles
- Identify and document roles, responsibilities, and measures of success per actor, the required scripts per actor, and the desired results of handling the situation properly
- Check for fitness-for-purpose of inspiring subsequent architecture work, and refine only if necessary

A list of example business scenarios available from The Open Group is given in Appendix B.

3.12 Technical Requirements

An initial set of Technical Requirements should be generated as the output of Phase B: Business Architecture. These are the drivers for the Technology Architecture work that follows, and should identify, categorize, and prioritize the implications for work in the remaining architecture domains.

3.13 Gap Analysis

The technique known as gap analysis is widely used in the TOGAF ADM to validate an architecture that is being developed. It is usually the final step within a phase. The basic premise is to highlight a shortfall between the Baseline Architecture and the Target Architecture; that is, items that have been deliberately omitted, accidentally left out, or not yet defined.

The steps are as follows:
- Draw up a matrix with all the Architecture Building Blocks (ABBs) of the Baseline Architecture on the vertical axis, and all the ABBs of the Target Architecture on the horizontal axis.
- Add to the Baseline Architecture axis a final row labeled "New ABBs", and to the Target Architecture axis a final column labeled "Eliminated ABBs".

- Where an ABB is available in both the Baseline and Target Architectures, record this with "Included" at the intersecting cell.
- Where an ABB from the Baseline Architecture is missing in the Target Architecture, each must be reviewed. If it was correctly eliminated, mark it as such in the appropriate "Eliminated" cell. If it was not, you have uncovered an accidental omission in your Target Architecture that must be addressed by reinstating the ABB in the next iteration of the architecture design – mark it as such in the appropriate "Eliminated" cell.
- Where an ABB from the Target Architecture cannot be found in the Baseline Architecture, mark it at the intersection with the "New" row as a gap that needs to filled, either by developing or procuring the building block.

When the exercise is complete, anything under "Eliminated Services" or "New Services" is a gap, which should either be explained as correctly eliminated, or marked as to be addressed by reinstating or developing/procuring the function.

Table 3.4 shows examples of gaps between the Baseline Architecture and the Target Architecture; in this case the missing elements are "broadcast services" and "shared screen services".

Table 3.4 Gap Analysis Example

Target Architecture → Baseline Architecture ↓	Video Conferencing Services	Enhanced Telephony Services	Mailing List Services	Eliminated Services ↓
Broadcast Services				Intentionally Eliminated
Video Conferencing Services	Included			
Enhanced Telephony Services		Potential Match		
Shared Screen Services				Unintentionally excluded – a gap in Target Architecture
New →		Gap: Enhanced services to be developed or produced	Gap: Enhanced services to be developed or produced	

It is recommended that the gap analysis technique be used in Phases B, C and D of the ADM.

3.14 Data Architecture

The objectives of Phase C are to produce the Data Architecture. It should comprise some or all of:

- Business data model
- Logical data model
- Data management process model

- Data entity/business function matrix
- Data interoperability requirements

3.15 Data Architecture Report

The Data Architecture Report produced in the Data Architecture part of Phase C summarizes the activities of the phase and the key findings (essentially providing a log of the activities in this phase).

3.16 Applications Architecture

The Applications Architecture is developed as part of Phase C.
Phase C includes a description of what should be defined as the Baseline Architecture description for each application, and also a description of what should be defined for all candidate applications within the Target Architecture.

3.17 Applications Architecture Report

This is an output of the Applications Architecture part of Phase C. This should include a summary of the tasks undertaken in this phase and the key recommendations.

3.18 Technology Architecture

The Technology Architecture is developed in Phase D. The topics that should be addressed in the Technology Architecture are as follows:
- Baseline Technology Architecture
- Objectives and constraints:
  - Technology requirements and key system and architecture drivers
  - Assumptions (e.g., business, financial, organizational, or required technical functionality)
- Technology Architecture model(s):
  - Architecture Building Block (ABB) models of views (minimally a model of functions and a model of services)
  - ABB models of service portfolios (enterprise-specific framework)
- Technology Architecture specification:

For each ABB produce:

- – Details of the technical functionality
- – A fully defined list of all the standards
- – A description of the building blocks at the levels necessary to support implementation, enterprise-wide strategic decision-making, and further iterations of the architecture definition process
- – Rationale for decisions taken that relate to the building block, including rationales for decisions not to do something
- – A specification for the building block identifying the interworking with other building blocks, including how
- – Guidelines for procuring
- – Standards summary list
- Requirements traceability
- Acceptance criteria:
  - – Criteria for choosing specifications
  - – Criteria for selection of portfolios of specifications
  - – Criteria to test merits of architecture (key question list)
  - – Report on cost/benefit analyses
  - – Report on how the proposed architecture meets the business goals and objectives
  - – Criteria response answers to key question list to test merits of architecture
- Gap report:
  - – Report on gap analysis
  - – Report of gap analysis matrix
- Mapping of the architectures in the Enterprise Continuum
- Change requests for extensions or amendments to related architectures

3.19 Technology Architecture Report

The Technology Architecture Report is produced as an output of Phase D: Technology Architecture. This should include a summary of the tasks undertaken in this phase and the key recommendations.

3.20 Architecture Viewpoints

The architect uses views and viewpoints in the ADM cycle during Phases
A through to D for developing architectures for each domain (Business,
Data, Applications, Technology). A "view" is what you see. A "viewpoint"
is where you are looking from; the vantage point or perspective that
determines what you see (a viewpoint can also be thought of as a schema).
Viewpoints are generic, and can be stored in libraries for re-use. A view is
always specific to the architecture for which it is created. Every view has an
associated viewpoint that describes it, at least implicitly.

ANSI/IEEE Std 1471-2000 encourages architects to define viewpoints
explicitly. Making this distinction between the content and schema of a
view may seem at first to be an unnecessary overhead, but it provides a
mechanism for re-using viewpoints across different architectures.

To illustrate the concepts of views and viewpoints, consider Example 3.1
that is a very simple airport system with two different stakeholders: the
pilot and the air traffic controller.

Example 3.1 Views and Viewpoints for a Simple Airport System

Views and Viewpoints for a Simple Airport System

The pilot has one view of the system, and the air traffic controller
has another. Neither view represents the whole system, because the
perspective of each stakeholder constrains (and reduces) how each sees
the overall system.

The view of the pilot comprises some elements not viewed by the
controller, such as passengers and fuel, while the view of the controller
comprises some elements not viewed by the pilot, such as other
planes. There are also elements shared between the views, such as the
communication model between the pilot and the controller, and the
vital information about the plane itself.

A viewpoint is a model (or description) of the information contained in a view. In this example, one viewpoint is the description of how the pilot sees the system, and the other viewpoint is how the controller sees the system. Pilots describe the system from their perspective, using a model of their position and vector toward or away from the runway. All pilots use this model, and the model has a specific language that is used to capture information and populate the model. Controllers describe the system differently, using a model of the airspace and the locations and vectors of aircraft within the airspace. Again, all controllers use a common language derived from the common model in order to capture and communicate information pertinent to their viewpoint. Fortunately, when controllers talk with pilots, they use a common communication language. (In other words, the models representing their individual viewpoints partially intersect.) Part of this common language is about location and vectors of aircraft, and is essential to safety. So in essence each viewpoint is an abstract model of how all the stakeholders of a particular type – all pilots, or all controllers – view the airport system. The interface to the human user of a tool is typically close to the model and language associated with the viewpoint. The unique tools of the pilot are fuel, altitude, speed, and location indicators. The main tool of the controller is radar. The common tool is a radio.

To summarize from Example 3.1, we can see that a view can subset the system through the perspective of the stakeholder, such as the pilot *versus* the controller. This subset can be described by an abstract model called a viewpoint, such as an air flight *versus* an air space model. This description of the view is documented in a partially specialized language, such as "pilot-speak" *versus* "controller-speak". Tools are used to assist the stakeholders, and they interface with each other in terms of the language derived from the viewpoint. When stakeholders use common tools, such as the radio contact between pilot and controller, a common language is essential.

3.21 Architecture Views

Architecture views are representations of the overall architecture that are meaningful to one or more stakeholders in the system. The architect chooses and develops a set of views in the ADM cycle during Phases A through to D that enable the architecture to be communicated to, and understood by, all the stakeholders, and enable them to verify that the system will address their concerns. The concepts in Table 3.5 are central to the use of architecture views within TOGAF.

3.21.1   Developing Views in the ADM

The choice of which particular architecture views to develop is one of the key decisions that the architect has to make.

The architect has a responsibility for ensuring the completeness (fitness-for-purpose) of the architecture, in terms of adequately addressing all the pertinent concerns of its stakeholders; and the integrity of the architecture, in terms of connecting all the various views to each other, satisfactorily reconciling the conflicting concerns of different stakeholders, and showing the trade-offs made in so doing (as between security and performance, for example).

3.22 Re-Usable Architecture Building Blocks

Re-usable Architecture Building Blocks (ABBs) are architecture documentation and models from the enterprise's Architecture Continuum. They are defined or selected during application of the ADM (mainly in Phases A, B, C, and D). The characteristics of ABBs are as follows:

- They define what functionality will be implemented.
- They capture business and technical requirements.
- They are technology-aware.
- They direct and guide the development of Solution Building Blocks.

Table 3.5 The Concepts Related to Architecture Views

Concept	Definition
System	A *system* is a collection of components organized to accomplish a specific function or set of functions.
Architecture	The *architecture* of a system is the system's fundamental organization, embodied in its components, their relationships to each other and to the environment, and the principles guiding its design and evolution.
Architecture Description	An *architecture description* is a collection of artifacts that document an architecture. In TOGAF, architecture views are the key artifacts in an architecture description.
Stakeholders	*Stakeholders* are people who have key roles in, or concerns about, the system; for example, as users, developers, or managers. Different stakeholders with different roles in the system will have different concerns. Stakeholders can be individuals, teams, or organizations (or classes thereof).
Concerns	*Concerns* are the key interests that are crucially important to the stakeholders in the system, and determine the acceptability of the system. Concerns may pertain to any aspect of the system's functioning, development, or operation, including considerations such as performance, reliability, security, distribution, and evolvability.
View	A *view* is a representation of a whole system from the perspective of a related set of concerns. In capturing or representing the design of a system's architecture, the architect will typically create one or more architecture models, possibly using different tools. A view will comprise selected parts of one or more models, chosen so as to demonstrate to a particular stakeholder or group of stakeholders that their concerns are being adequately addressed in the design of the system architecture.
Viewpoint	A *viewpoint* defines the perspective from which a view is taken. More specifically, a viewpoint defines: how to construct and use a view (by means of an appropriate schema or template); the information that should appear in the view; the modeling techniques for expressing and analyzing the information; and a rationale for these choices (e.g., by describing the purpose and intended audience of the view).

The content of ABB specifications includes the following as a minimum:

- Fundamental functionality and attributes: semantics, unambiguous, including security capability and manageability
- Interfaces: chosen set, supplied (APIs, data formats, protocols, hardware interfaces, standards)
- Dependent building blocks with required functionality and named user interfaces
- Map to business/organizational entities and policies

Each ABB should include a statement of any architecture documentation and models from the enterprise's Architecture Continuum that can be re-used in the architecture development. The specification of building blocks using the ADM is an evolutionary and iterative process. The key phases and steps of the ADM at which building blocks are evolved and specified are summarized below, and illustrated in Figure 3.1.

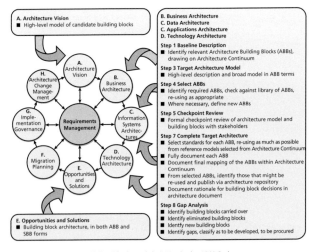

Figure 3.1 Architecture Building Blocks and their Use in the ADM Cycle

In Phase A, the earliest building block definitions start as relatively abstract entities within the Architecture Vision.

In Phases B, C, and D building blocks within the Business, Data, Applications, and Technology Architectures are evolved to a common pattern of steps:

- Step 1: Baseline Description produces a list of candidate building blocks, from the analysis of the baseline.
- Step 3: Target Architecture Model takes this list and high-level model as inputs, and evolves them iteratively into a definition of the Target Architecture, specified in terms of ABBs. Step 3 produces a high-level description and broad model of the target system in terms of ABBs and a rationale for each building block decision.
- Step 4: Select ABBs produces for each ABB a service description portfolio, built up as a set of non-conflicting services.
- Step 5: Checkpoint Review of the business goals and objectives produces confirmation of the merit and completeness of the model and service description portfolio, and a description of how the emerging Target Architecture meets the objectives of the architecture development.
- Step 7: Complete the Target Architecture fully specified in terms of ABBs, a fully defined (by service) list of all the standards that make up the Target Architecture, and all the ABBs that will be used to implement it, and a diagrammatic depiction of the building blocks at the levels needed to describe the strategic and implementation aspects of the architecture.
- Step 8: Gap Analysis produces a gap analysis report of the eliminated building blocks, carried over building blocks, and new building blocks.

Finally, in Phase E the building blocks become more implementation-specific as SBBs, and their interfaces become the detailed architecture specification. The output of Phase E is the building block architecture, both in ABB (i.e., functionally defined) and SBB (i.e., product-specific) forms.

3.23 Re-Usable Solution Building Blocks

Re-usable Solution Building Blocks (SBBs) relate to the Solutions Continuum. They are implementations of the architectures identified in the enterprise's Architecture Continuum and may be either procured or developed. SBBs appear in Phase E of the ADM where product-specific building blocks are considered for the first time. SBBs define what products and components will implement the functionality, thereby defining the implementation. They fulfill business requirements and are product or vendor-aware. The content of an SBB specification includes the following as a minimum:

- Specific functionality and attributes
- Interfaces; the implemented set
- Required SBBs used with required functionality and names of the interfaces used
- Mapping from the SBBs to the IT topology and operational policies
- Specifications of attributes shared such as security, manageability, localizability, scalability
- Performance, configurability
- Design drivers and constraints, including the physical architecture
- Relationships between the SBBs and ABBs

3.24 Impact Analysis Document – Project List

The Impact Analysis document is a document generated in Phases E, F, and G. Each phase updates the document. Phase E: Opportunities and Solutions adds the project list to the Impact Analysis document. It identifies possible work packages or projects, together with classifications and priorities. The recommended contents for the project list include the name, description, and objectives of each impacted project, together with a prioritized list of impacted projects to implement the proposed architecture.

3.25 Impact Analysis Document – Migration Plan

Phase F: Migration Planning adds the Migration Plan to the Impact Analysis document. This documents how existing systems will be migrated to the new architecture. The recommended contents for a Migration Plan should address the benefits of migration (including mapping to business requirements), together with the estimated costs of the migration options.

3.26 Impact Analysis Document – Implementation Recommendations

Phase G: Implementation Governance adds the implementation recommendations to the Impact Analysis document. The recommended contents for Implementation Recommendations should include criteria measures for the effectiveness of the projects, identified risks and issues, and a description and model of the Solution Building Blocks.

3.27 Architecture Contracts

Architecture Contracts are produced in Phase G: Implementation Governance. Typical contents of an Architecture Design and Development Contract are:

- Introduction and background
- The nature of the agreement
- Scope of the architecture
- Architecture and strategic principles and requirements
- Conformance requirements
- Architecture development and management process and roles
- Target architecture measures
- Defined phases of deliverables
- Prioritized joint workplan

- Time window(s)
- Architecture delivery and business metrics

Typical contents of a Business Users' Architecture Contract produced in Phase G are:
- Introduction and background
- The nature of the agreement
- Scope
- Strategic requirements
- Conformance requirements
- Architecture adopters
- Time window
- Architecture business metrics
- Service architecture (includes Service Level Agreement (SLA))

This contract is also used to manage changes to the enterprise architecture in Phase H.

3.28 Product Information

Product information is an input to Phase E: Opportunities and Solutions. Where there are product implementations that are candidates for the architecture implementation, then a document should be produced containing functional descriptions of the candidate products, together with architecture descriptions of the candidate elements.

3.29 Request for Architecture Change

According to Phase H, Requests for Architecture Change are driven by technology changes or business changes. TOGAF provides a set of guidelines for reviewing Requests for Architecture Change to enable a controlled and consistent change management process.

3.30 New Technology Reports

New technology reports are generated in Phase H and drive the Change
Management process. These should document new developments in
potentially relevant technology. There is no recommended format for
them.

3.31 Requirements Impact Statement

This is an output of Phase H and is a response to a Request for
Architecture Change. It documents an assessment of the changes and
the recommendations for change to the architecture. The recommended
contents are as follows:

- Reference to specific requirements
- Stakeholder priority of the requirements to date
- Phases to be revisited
- Phase to lead on requirements prioritization
- Results of phase investigations and revised priorities
- Recommendations on management of requirements
- Repository reference number

Chapter 4
The Enterprise Continuum

This chapter provides an introduction to the Enterprise Continuum.
Topics addressed in this chapter include:

- An explanation of the Enterprise Continuum and its purpose
- Using the Enterprise Continuum in developing an enterprise architecture
- An introduction to the two example architectures included in the TOGAF 8.1.1 Enterprise Continuum

4.1 Overview of the Enterprise Continuum

The Enterprise Continuum, shown in Figure 4.1, provides a model for structuring a "virtual" repository that can be filled with architecture assets and their possible solutions (models, patterns, architecture descriptions, etc.). These assets and solutions can be drawn from within the enterprise or from the industry at large and used in constructing architectures.

A distinction is made between architectures and their possible solutions, thus creating an Architecture Continuum and a Solutions Continuum. As shown in Figure 4.1, the relationship between them is one of guidance, direction and support.

The Enterprise Continuum supports two general ideas: re-use where possible, especially the avoidance of reinvention, and an aid to communication. The assets in both the Architecture and Solutions Continuums are structured from generic to specific in order to provide a consistent language to communicate effectively over the differences between architectures. Knowing "where in the continuum you are", avoids people talking at cross-purposes. Use of the Enterprise Continuum can eliminate ambiguity when discussing concepts and items amongst different

Architecture Continuum

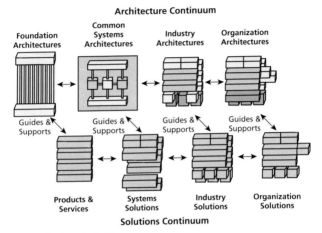

Figure 4.1 The Enterprise Continuum

departments within the same organization or even different organizations constructing enterprise architectures. Understanding the architecture on which a solution is based helps understanding the solution itself. Being able to explain the general concept behind a specific solution makes it easier to understand possible conflicts.

By using the Enterprise Continuum the set of relevant architecture and solution assets will grow so the organization can benefit from re-use. At relevant places throughout the TOGAF ADM, there are reminders to consider which architecture assets the architect should use.

4.1.1 The Enterprise Continuum and Architecture Re-Use

Examples of assets "within the enterprise" are the deliverables of previous architecture work, which are available for re-use. Examples of assets "in the IT industry at large" are the wide variety of industry reference models and architecture patterns that exist, and are continually emerging, including those that are highly generic (such as TOGAF's own Technical Reference Model (TRM)); those specific to certain aspects of IT (such as a web services architecture); those specific to certain types of information processing (such as e-Commerce); and those specific to certain vertical industries (such as the ARTS data model from the retail industry). The decision as to which architecture assets a specific enterprise considers part of its own Enterprise Continuum will normally form part of the overall architecture governance function within the enterprise concerned.

4.1.2 Using the Enterprise Continuum within the ADM

In the TOGAF Architecture Development Method (ADM) a process of moving from the TOGAF Foundation Architecture to an enterprise-specific architecture (or set of architectures) is described. This Foundation Architecture is a highly general description of generic services and functions that provide the foundation on which specific architectures and architectural building blocks can be built by adding relevant architecture assets, components, and building blocks from the Enterprise Continuum. At relevant places throughout the TOGAF ADM, there are reminders to consider which architecture assets the architect should use. In addition to the TOGAF Foundation Architecture TOGAF provides another reference model for consideration for inclusion in an organization's Enterprise Continuum: the Integrated Information Infrastructure Reference Model (III-RM).

4.2 Introduction to the TOGAF Foundation Architecture

A Foundation Architecture is defined as follows:

"An architecture of building blocks and corresponding standards that supports all the Common Systems Architectures and, therefore, the complete computing environment."

The TOGAF Foundation Architecture is an architecture that provides a foundation on which specific architectures and Architecture Building Blocks (ABBs) can be built. It comprises the Technical Reference Model (TRM) and the Standards Information Base (SIB).

The TRM, shown in Figure 4.2, is a model and taxonomy of generic platform services. The taxonomy defines the terminology and provides a coherent description of its components. Its purpose is to give a conceptual description of an Information System. And the TRM model is a graphical representation of the taxonomy to act as an aid for understanding.

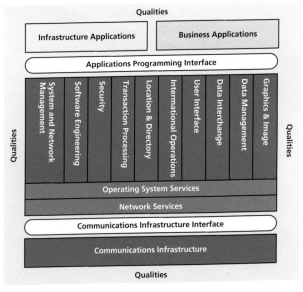

Figure 4.2 The TRM

The SIB is a database of open industry standards that can be used to define the particular services and other components of an Enterprise Architecture.

4.3 The Integrated Information Infrastructure Reference Model (III-RM)

Whereas the Foundation Architecture describes a typical application platform environment the second reference model included in the Enterprise Continuum, the Integrated Information Infrastructure Reference Model (III-RM), focuses on the application software space. The III-RM is a "Common Systems Architecture" in Enterprise Continuum terms.

The III-RM is shown in Figure 4.3 and is a subset of the TOGAF TRM in terms of its overall scope, but it also expands certain parts of the TRM in particular in the business applications and infrastructure applications parts. The III-RM provides help in addressing one of the key challenges facing the enterprise architect today: the need to design an integrated information infrastructure to enable Boundaryless Information Flow.

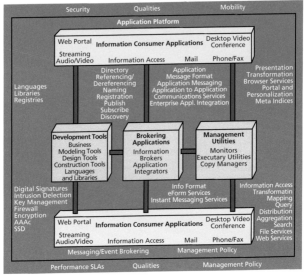

Figure 4.3 The III-RM in Detail

Chapter 5
The TOGAF Resource Base

This chapter provides an introduction to the Resource Base that comprises Part IV of TOGAF.

5.1 Introduction to the Resource Base

The Resource Base is a set of resources, guidelines, processes, checklists, templates, and background information provided to be of assistance to the architect in the use of TOGAF and the ADM. Some parts of the Resource Base also have an applicability beyond just use with TOGAF – for example, the Skills Framework – and provide resources that are of use to all enterprise architecture projects.

In TOGAF 8.1.1 the Resource Base is organized as seventeen separate chapters addressing distinct topics that can be summarized in the following themes (shown in the following table) that are then expanded in the subsequent part of this chapter.

Theme	Resource Base Chapters
Governance and Design Authority	Architecture Board: Guidelines for establishing and operating an enterprise Architecture Board.
	Architecture Compliance: Guidelines for ensuring project compliance to architecture.
	Architecture Contracts: Guidelines for defining and using Architecture Contracts.
	Architecture Governance: Framework and guidelines for architecture governance.

Theme	Resource Base Chapters
Models	Architecture Maturity Models: Techniques for evaluating and quantifying an organization's maturity in enterprise architecture. Architecture Views: Guidelines for viewpoints and views in architecture models. Building Blocks Example: A fictional example illustrating building blocks in architecture. Business Process Domain Views: A set of function views aligned with the business process structure of the enterprise. Architecture Patterns: Guidelines for using architectural patterns.
Methods, Tools, and Techniques	Architecture Principles: Principles for the use and deployment of IT resources across the enterprise. Tools for Architecture Development: Tools and techniques helpful in using TOGAF. Business Scenarios: A method for deriving business requirements for architecture and the implied technical requirements.
Architecture Practice	Architecture Skills Framework: A set of role, skill, and experience norms for staff undertaking enterprise architecture work. Case Studies: Real-life examples of TOGAF in use.
Other Frameworks	Other Architectures/Frameworks: Other frameworks and their relationship to TOGAF. Zachman Framework Mapping: Mapping the TOGAF ADM to the Zachman Framework.
Definitions	Glossary: Definitions of key terms.

5.2 Governance and Design Authority

5.2.1 Architecture Board

An enterprise architecture is more than just the artefacts produced by the application of the ADM process. Making the organization act according to the principles laid down in the architecture requires a decision-making framework around it. The Resource Base provides a set of guidelines for establishing and operating an enterprise Architecture Board. An Architecture Board is responsible for operational items and must be capable of making decisions in situations of possible conflict and accountable for taking those decisions. It should therefore be a representation of all the key stakeholders in the architecture, and will typically comprise a group of executives responsible for the review and maintenance of the overall architecture. It is important that the members of the Architecture Board cover architecture, business and program management areas.

Issues the Architecture Board can be made responsible and accountable for are:

- Consistency between sub-architectures
- Identifying re-usable components
- Flexibility of enterprise architecture; to meet business needs and utilize new technologies
- Enforcement of Architecture Compliance
- Improving the maturity level of architecture discipline within the organization
- Ensuring that the discipline of architecture-based development is adopted
- Providing the basis for all decision-making with regard to changes to the architectures
- Supporting a visible escalation capability for out-of-bounds decisions

The Architecture Board is also responsible for operational items such as the monitoring and control of Architecture Contracts, and for governance items such as producing usable governance materials. Important tasks are:

- Assigning architectural tasks
- Formally approving architectural products
- Resolving architectural conflicts

5.2.2 Architecture Compliance

Using architecture to structure IT development in an organization implies that IT-projects should comply with the planned architecture roadmap. If that's not the case, then there must be a good reason for it.

To determine whether this is the case, an Architecture Compliance strategy should be adopted with specific measures to ensure compliance with the architecture. The Resource Base includes a set of processes, guidelines and a checklist for ensuring project compliance to the architecture, including:

- Project Impact Assessments that illustrate how the enterprise architecture impacts on the major projects within an organization
- The Architecture Compliance Review process, which is a formal process for reviewing the compliance of projects to the enterprise architecture

5.2.3 Architecture Contracts

The Resource Base includes a set of guidelines for defining and using Architecture Contracts.

Architecture Contracts are the joint agreements between development partners and sponsors on the deliverables, quality, and fitness-for-purpose of an architecture. Adhering to these contracts makes architecture effective. Concluding these contracts makes governing the architecture possible, as well as adherence to the principles, standards, and requirements of the enterprise.

5.2.4 Architecture Governance

The Resource Base contains a framework and guidelines for architecture governance. Architecture governance is the practice by which enterprise architectures and other architectures are managed and controlled at an enterprise-wide level. It includes the following:

- Implementing a system of controls over the creation and monitoring of all architecture components and activities, to ensure the effective introduction, implementation, and evolution of architectures within the organization

- Implementing a system to ensure compliance with internal and external standards and regulatory obligations
- Establishing processes that support effective management of the above processes within agreed parameters
- Establishing and documenting decision structures that influence the enterprise architecture; this includes stakeholders that provide input to decisions
- Developing practices that ensure accountability to a clearly identified stakeholder community, both inside and outside the organization

5.3   Models

5.3.1 Architecture Maturity Models

The Resource Base contains information on a set of techniques for evaluating and quantifying an organization's maturity in enterprise architecture. This section introduces the topic of capability maturity models and their associated methods and techniques, as a widely used industry standard that is mature enough to consider for use in relation to enterprise architecture.

A maturity model characterizes an organization's maturity in different levels and for different processes. These levels generally range from non-existent to optimized in different subsequent steps. Evaluating an organization against these levels, called an assessment, indicates the current level of maturity and provides a suggestion for action to reach the next level of maturity. The descriptions of these maturity levels are based on best practice and consensus. They assume that every organization follows the same path to success.

5.3.2 Architecture Patterns

The Resource Base contains a set of guidelines for using architectural patterns.

Patterns for system architecting are very much in their infancy. They have been introduced into TOGAF essentially to draw them to the attention of the systems architecture community as an emerging important resource, and as a placeholder for hopefully more rigorous descriptions and references to more plentiful resources in future versions of TOGAF.

5.3.3 Architecture Views

The Resource Base contains a set of guidelines for developing and using viewpoints and views in architecture models.

The architect uses views and viewpoints in the ADM cycle during Phases A through to D for developing architectures for each domain (Business, Data, Applications, Technology). A "view" is what you see. A "viewpoint" is where you are looking from; the vantage point or perspective that determines what you see (a viewpoint can also be thought of as a schema). Viewpoints are generic, and can be stored in libraries for re-use. A view is always specific to the architecture for which it is created. Every view has an associated viewpoint that describes it, at least implicitly. See Section 3.21 for more information.

5.3.4 Building Blocks

The Resource Base explains the concept of building blocks together with a fictional example illustrating building blocks in architecture. TOGAF includes Architecture Building Blocks (ABBs) and Solution Building Blocks (SBBs).

Building blocks is a pervasive term within TOGAF and the ADM. A building block is simply a package of functionality defined to meet business needs. The way in which functionality, products, and custom developments are assembled into building blocks will vary widely between individual architectures. Every organization must decide for itself what arrangement of building blocks works best for it. A good choice of building blocks can lead to improvements in legacy system integration, interoperability, and flexibility in the creation of new systems and applications.

Systems are built up from collections of building blocks, so most building blocks have to interoperate with other building blocks. Wherever that is true, it is important that the interfaces to a building block are published and reasonably stable.

Building blocks can be defined at various levels of detail, depending on what stage of architecture development has been reached.

For instance, at an early stage, a building block can simply consist of a grouping of functionality, such as a customer database and some retrieval tools. Building blocks at this functional level of definition are described in TOGAF as Architecture Building Blocks (ABBs). Later on, real products or specific custom developments replace these simple definitions of functionality, and the building blocks are then described as Solution Building Blocks (SBBs).

5.3.5 Business Process Domain Views

The Resource Base includes a set of function views aligned with the business process structure of the enterprise.

A business process domain is a logical grouping of business systems dedicated to a common purpose. Such systems may be geographically co-located, thus emphasizing their purpose; or they may be grouped by some other constraint, such as a common systems availability target.

In order to demonstrate the responsiveness of the enterprise architecture to the business needs of the organization, among the various architecture views that are developed, a business process domain view may be used.

This describes the enterprise architecture from the perspective of the enterprise's key business process domains.

5.4   Methods, Tools, and Techniques

5.4.1 Architecture Principles

The Resource Base contains a set of principles for the use and deployment of IT resources across the enterprise.

Principles are general rules and guidelines, intended to be enduring and seldom amended, which inform and support the way in which an organization sets about fulfilling its mission. In their turn, principles may be just one element in a structured set of ideas that collectively define and guide the organization, from values through to actions and results.

See Section 3.2 for more information.

5.4.2 Business Scenarios

The Resource Base documents a technique known as a *business scenario*. See Section 3.11 for more information.

5.4.3 Tools for Architecture Development

This part of the Resource Base discusses tools and techniques helpful in using TOGAF.

5.5   Architecture Practice

5.5.1 Architecture Skills Framework

The Resource Base provides a set of role, skill, and experience norms for staff undertaking enterprise architecture work.

"IT Architecture" and "IT Architect" are widely used but poorly defined terms in the IT industry today. They are used to denote a variety of practices and skills applied in a wide variety of IT domains. There is a need for better classification to enable more implicit understanding of what type of architect/architecture is being described.

This lack of uniformity leads to difficulties for organizations seeking to recruit or assign/promote staff to fill positions in the architecture field. Because of the different usages of terms, there is often misunderstanding and miscommunication between those seeking to recruit for, and those seeking to fill, the various roles of the architect.

The TOGAF Architecture Skills Framework attempts to address this need by providing definitions of the architecting skills and proficiency levels required of personnel, internal or external, who are to perform the various architecting roles defined within the TOGAF Framework.

5.5.2 Case Studies

This part of the Resource Base contains a number of case studies of uses of TOGAF.

5.6   Other Frameworks

A number of architecture frameworks exist, each of which has its particular advantages and disadvantages, and relevance, for enterprise architecture. However, there is no accepted industry standard method for developing an enterprise architecture. The Open Group goal with TOGAF is to work towards making the TOGAF ADM just such an industry standard method, which can be used for developing the products associated with any recognized enterprise framework that the architect feels is appropriate for a particular architecture. The Open Group vision for TOGAF is as a vehicle and repository for practical, experience-based information on how to go about the process of enterprise architecture, providing a generic method with which specific sets of deliverables, specific reference models, and other relevant architectural assets can be integrated.

To this aim, the Resource Base includes two chapters in this theme. Additional information is also available in the TOGAF White Papers (see Section B.2).

5.6.1 Other Frameworks and their Relationship to TOGAF

TOGAF is one of a number of architectures and architecture frameworks in use today. Many of the other architecture initiatives have a good deal in common with TOGAF. This part of the Resource Base describes these initiatives and explains the relationship, if any, to TOGAF.

5.6.2 Zachman Framework Mapping

This part of the Resource Base provides a mapping of the phases of the TOGAF ADM to the cells of the Zachman Framework.

5.7 Definitions and Terms

5.7.1 Glossary

The TOGAF Glossary is intended to define terms essential to the understanding of TOGAF. It is not intended as a general-purpose open systems glossary and does not contain terms considered to be in common use.

Appendix A
Guidelines on Developing Business Scenarios

A.1   Introduction

A key factor in the success of developing an enterprise architecture, or any other major project, is the extent to which it is linked to business requirements, and demonstrably supports and enables the enterprise to achieve its business objectives.

Business Scenarios were developed as part of The Open Group Architecture Framework (TOGAF), in order to quantify and document business processes. As well as playing a key part in defining and developing an enterprise architecture, Business Scenarios have value as a tool in their own right. This appendix is an abridged portion of Doc. No. G261,[5] which provides guidelines for developing Business Scenarios. You do not need to be developing an architecture (though that always improves the prospect of a successful outcome for an IT project) in order to derive value from Business Scenarios.

A.2   General Guidelines

The stakeholders (e.g., business managers, end-users) may well be able to describe what they need, but often that is not the case. In order to gain a complete understanding of the business, you must identify the most important actors in the system.

---

5   Manager's Guide to Business Scenarios (ISBN: 1-931624-15-1, G261), available at www.opengroup.org/bookstore/catalog/g261.htm.

If the stakeholders do not know what they want:
- Take time to observe and record how they are working today
- Structure information so that it can be used later
- Uncover critical business rules from domain experts
- Stay focused on what needs to be accomplished and how it is to be accomplished

This effort provides the anchor for a chain of reason, from business requirements through to technical solutions. Being diligent and critical at the start will pay off later.

A good Business Scenario should be "SMART":
- **S**pecific, by defining what needs to be done in the business
- **M**easurable, through clear metrics for success
- **A**ctionable, by:
  - Clearly segmenting the problem
  - Providing the basis for determining elements and plans for the solution
- **R**ealistic, in that the problem can be solved within the bounds of physical reality, time and cost constraints
- **T**ime-sensitive, in that there is a clear statement of when the solution opportunity expires

A.3   Questions to Ask for Each Area

The Business Scenario workshops in the Gathering phase are really structured interviews. While there is no single set of appropriate questions to ask in all situations, the following provides some guidance to help Business Scenario consultants ask good questions.

Identifying, Documenting, and Ranking the Problem

Is the problem described as a statement of WHAT needs to be accomplished, like steps in a process, and not HOW (with technology "push")?

If the problem is too specific or a "how":
- Raise a red flag
- Ask questions, such as: "Why do you need to do it that way?"

If the problem is too vague or unactionable:
- Raise a red flag
- Ask questions, such as: "What is it you need to do?" "What will you be able to do if this problem is solved?"

Ask questions that help identify where and when the problem exists:
- Where are you experiencing this particular problem? In what business process?
- When do you encounter these issues? During the beginning of the process, the middle, the end?

Ask questions that help identify the costs of the problem:
- Do you account for the costs associated with this problem? If so, what are they?
- Are there hidden costs? If so, what are they?
- Is the cost of this problem covered in the cost of something else? If so, what and how much?
- Is the problem manifested in terms of poor quality or a perception of an ineffective organization?

Identifying the Business and Technical Environment and Documenting in Models

Questions to ask about the business environment:
- What key processes suffer from the issues? What are the major steps that need to be processed?
- Location/scale of internal business departments?
- Location/scale of external business partners?
- Any specific business rules and regulations related to the situation?

Questions to ask about the current technology environment:

- What technology components are already pre-supposed to be related to this problem?
- Are there any technology constraints?
- Are there any technology principles that apply?

Identifying and Documenting Objectives

Is the "what" sufficiently backed up with the rationale for "why"? If not, ask for measurable rationale in the following areas:

- Return on investment
- Scalability
- Performance needs
- Compliance to standards
- Ease-of-use measures

Identifying Human Actors and their Place in the Business Model

An actor represents anything that interacts with or within the system. This can be a human or a machine or a computer program. Actors initiate activity with the system; for example:

- Computer user with the computer
- Phone user with the telephone
- Payroll clerk with the payroll system
- Internet subscriber with the web browser

An actor represents a role that a user plays. In other words, a user is someone playing a role while using the system; e.g., John (user) is a dispatcher (actor). Each actor uses the system in different ways (otherwise they should be identified as the same actor). Ask about the humans who will be involved, from different viewpoints, such as:

- Developer
- Maintainer
- Operator

- Administrator
- User

Identifying Computer Actors and their Place in the Technology Model
Ask about the computer components likely to be involved, again from different points of view. What must they do?

Documenting Roles, Responsibilities, Measures of Success, Required Scripts
When defining roles, ask questions such as:
- What are the main tasks of the actor?
- Will the actor have to read/write/change any information?
- Will the actor have to inform the system about outside changes?
- Does the actor wish to be informed about unexpected changes?

Checking for Fitness-for-Purpose and Refining, if necessary
Is there enough information to identify who/what could fulfill the requirement? If not, probe more deeply.

Is there a description of when and how often the requirement needs to be addressed? If not, ask about timing.

A.4 Guidelines on Business Scenario Documentation

Textual Documentation
Documentation must be effective. This requires a balance of ensuring that the detail is accessible, but that it does not overshadow the results or overwhelm the reader. To accomplish this, the generalized findings should be in the main body of the Business Scenarios document and the details should be covered in appendices.

Capture all the important details about a Business Scenario and put them in appendices:

- Situation description and rationale
- All measurements
- All actor roles and sub-measurements
- All services required
- Critical steps between actors that address the situation and sequence the interactions
- Relevant information about all actors
  - Partition the responsibility of the actors
  - List pre-conditions that have to be met prior to proper system functionality
  - Provide technical requirements for the service to be of acceptable quality

Generalize all the relevant data from the detail and document the generalizations in the main body of the Business Scenario document.

Business Scenario Models
Business Scenario models are fundamentally pictures. As they say, a picture is worth a thousand words. The purpose of using models is to:

- Capture business and technology views in a graphical form
- Aid in comprehension
- Provide a starting point for confirming requirements
- Relate actors and interactions

To achieve the objectives of using models:

- Keep drawings clear and neat
- Avoid putting too much detail in one diagram; simpler diagrams are easier to understand
- Number the models for easy reference

A.5   Guidelines on Goals and Objectives

The Importance of Goals

One of the first steps in the development of an architecture is to define the overall goals and objectives for the development. The objectives should be derived from the business goals of the organization, and the way in which information technology is seen to contribute to meeting those goals should be clear.

Every organization behaves differently in this respect, some seeing IT as the driving force for the enterprise and others seeing IT in a supporting role, simply automating the business processes that already exist. It is essential that the architectural objectives be very closely aligned with the business goals and objectives of the organization.

The Importance of SMART Objectives

Not only must goals be stated in general terms, but also specific measures need to be attached to them to make them SMART, as described earlier. The amount of effort spent in doing this will lead to greater clarity for the sponsors of the architecture evolution cycle. It will pay off by driving proposed solutions much closer to the goals, at each step of the cycle. It is extremely helpful for the different stakeholders inside the organization, as well as for suppliers and consultants, to have a clear yardstick for measuring fitness-for-purpose. If done well, the architecture development method can be used to trace specific decisions back to criteria, thus yielding their justification.

The goals below have been adapted from experience in developing previous scenarios. These are categories of goals, each with a list of possible objectives. Each of these objectives should be made SMART, with specific measures and metrics for the task. However, since the actual work to be done will be specific to the architecture project concerned, it is not possible to provide a list of generic SMART objectives that will relate to every project.

Instead, we provide here some example SMART objectives.

Examples of Making Objectives SMART

Under the following general goal heading "Improve User Productivity", there is an objective to provide a "consistent user interface". It is described like this:

"A consistent user interface will ensure that all user-accessible functions and services will appear and behave in a similar, predictable fashion, regardless of application or site. This will lead to better efficiency and fewer user errors which, in turn, may result in lower recovery costs."

To make this objective SMART, we ask whether the objective is specific, measurable, actionable, realistic and time-bound, and if it augments the objective appropriately.

The following captures an analysis of these criteria for the stated objective:

- Specific – The objective of providing "a consistent user interface that will ensure all user-accessible functions and services will appear and behave in a similar, predictable fashion regardless of application or site" is pretty specific. However, the measures listed in the second sentence could be more specific.

- Measurable – As stated above, the objective is measurable, but could be more specific. The second sentence could be amended to read (for example): "This will lead to 10% greater user efficiency and 20% fewer order-entry user errors which, in turn, may result in 5% lower order-entry costs."

- Actionable – The objective does appear to be actionable. It seems clear that consistency of the user interface must be provided and could be handled by whoever is responsible for providing the user interface to the user device.

- Realistic – The objective of providing "a consistent user interface that will ensure all user-accessible functions and services will appear and behave in a similar, predictable fashion regardless of application or site" might not be realistic. Considering the use of PDAs today, at the user end, might lead us to augment this objective to ensure that the downstream developers don't unduly create designs that hinder the use of new technologies. The objective could be re-stated as "a consistent user interface, across user-interface devices that provide similar functionality, to ensure ..." etc.

- Time-bound – the objective as stated is not time-bound. To be time-bound the objective could be re-stated as "By the end of Quarter 3, provide a consistent…."

Putting all of the above together results in a SMART objective that reads more like this (again remember this is an example):

"By the end of Quarter 3, provide a consistent user interface across user-interface devices that provide similar functionality, to ensure all user-accessible functions and services appear and behave in a similar manner when using those devices in a predictable fashion, regardless of application or site. This will lead to 10% greater user efficiency and 20% fewer order-entry user errors which, in turn, may result in 5% lower order-entry costs."

Categories of Goals and Objectives

Although every organization will have its own set of goals, some examples may help in the development of an organization-specific list. The goals given below are categories of goals, each with a list of possible objectives, which have been adapted from the goals given in previous versions of TOGAF.

Each of the objectives given below should be made SMART with specific measures and metrics for the task involved, as illustrated in the preceding example. However, the actual work to be done will be specific to the architecture project concerned. It is not possible to provide a list of generic SMART objectives that will relate to every project.

Goal: Improve business process performance

Business process improvements can be realized through the following objectives:

- Increased process throughput
- Consistent output quality
- Predictable process costs
- Increased re-use of existing processes
- Reduced time sending business information from one process to another

Goal: Decrease costs

Cost reductions can be realized through the following objectives:

- Reduced levels of redundancy and duplication in assets throughout the enterprise
- Decreased reliance on external IT service providers for integration and customization
- Reduced costs of maintenance

Goal: Improve business operations

Business operations improvements can be realized through the following objectives:

- Increased budget available for new business features
- Reduced costs of running the business
- Shorter time-to-market for products or services
- Improved quality of services to customers
- Improved quality of business information

Goal: Improve management efficacy

Management efficacy improvements can be realized through the following objectives:

- Increased flexibility of business
- Shorter time to make decisions
- Better quality decisions

Goal: Reduce risk

Risk reductions can be realized through the following objectives:
- Ease of implementing new processes
- Fewer errors introduced into business processes through complex and faulty systems
- Fewer real-world safety hazards (including hazards that cause loss of life)

Goal: Improve effectiveness of IT organization

IT organization effectiveness can be improved through the following objectives:
- Increased number of new projects
- Shorter time to rollout new projects
- Reduced costs for rolling out new projects
- Reduced loss-of-service continuity when rolling out new projects
- Common development – Applications that are common to multiple business areas will be developed or acquired once and re-used, rather than separately developed by each business area.
- Open systems environment – A standards-based common operating environment that accommodates the injection of new standards, technologies and applications on an organization-wide basis will be established. This standards-based environment will provide the basis for development of common applications and facilitate software re-use.
- Use of products – As far as possible, hardware-independent, off-the-shelf items should be used to satisfy requirements in order to reduce dependence on custom developments and to reduce development and maintenance costs.
- Software re-use – For those applications that must be custom developed, development of portable applications will reduce the amount of software

developed and add to the inventory of software suitable for re-use by other systems.

- Resource sharing – Data-processing resources (hardware, software and data) will be shared by all users requiring the services of those resources. Resource sharing will be accomplished in the context of security and operational considerations.

Goal: Improve user productivity

User productivity improvements can be realized through the following objectives:

- Consistent user interface – A consistent user interface will ensure that all user-accessible functions and services will appear and behave in a similar, predictable fashion regardless of application or site. This will lead to better efficiency and fewer user errors which, in turn, may result in lower recovery costs.
- Integrated applications – Applications available to the user will behave in a logically consistent manner across user environments, which will lead to the same benefits as a consistent user interface.
- Data sharing – Databases will be shared across the organization in the context of security and operational considerations, leading to increased ease of access to required data.

Goal: Improve portability and scalability

The portability and scalability of applications will be realized through the following objectives:

- Portability – Applications that adhere to open systems standards will be portable, leading to ease of movement across heterogeneous computing platforms. Portable applications can allow sites to upgrade their platforms as technological improvements occur, with minimal impact on operations.

- Scalability – Applications that conform to the model will be configurable, allowing operation on the full spectrum of platforms required.

Goal: Improve interoperability

Interoperability improvements across applications and business areas can be realized through the following objectives:

- Common infrastructure – The architecture should promote a communications and computing infrastructure based on open systems and systems transparency including, but not limited to, operating systems, database management, data interchange, network services, network management and user interfaces.
- Standardization – By implementing standards-based platforms, applications will be provided with and will be able to use a common set of services that improve the opportunities for interoperability.

Goal: Increase vendor independence

Vendor independence can be increased through the following objectives:

- Interchangeable components – Only hardware and software that have standards-based interfaces will be selected, so that upgrades or the insertion of new products will result in minimal disruption to the user's environment.
- Non-proprietary specifications – Capabilities will be defined in terms of non-proprietary specifications that support full and open competition and are available to any vendor for use in developing commercial products.

Goal: Reduce lifecycle costs

Lifecycle costs can be reduced through most of the objectives identified above. In addition, the following objectives directly address reduction of lifecycle costs:

- Reduced duplication – Replacement of isolated systems and islands of automation with interconnected open systems will lead to reductions in overlapping functionality, data duplication, and unnecessary redundancy, because open systems can share data and other resources.
- Reduced software maintenance costs – Reductions in the quantity and variety of software used in the organization will lead to reductions in the amount and cost of software maintenance. Use of standard, off-the-shelf software will lead to further reductions in costs since vendors of such software distribute their product-maintenance costs across a much larger user base.
- Incremental replacement – Interfaces common to shared infrastructure components allow for phased replacement or upgrade with minimal operational disturbance.
- Reduced training costs – Common systems and consistent human computer interfaces will lead to reduced training costs.

Goal: Improve security

Security can be improved in the organization's information systems through the following objectives:

- Consistent security interfaces for applications – Consistent security interfaces and procedures will lead to fewer errors when developing applications, as well as to increased application portability. Not all applications will need the same suite of security features, but any features used will be consistent across applications.
- Consistent security interfaces for users – A common user interface for security features will lead to reduced learning time when moving from system to system.

- Security independence – Application deployment can use the security policy and mechanisms appropriate to the particular environment, if there is good layering in the architecture.
- A 25% reduction in calls to the Help desk relating to security issues.
- A 20% reduction in "false positives" detected in the network (a "false positive" is an event that appears to be an actionable security event but is in fact, is a false alarm).

Goal: Improve manageability

Management improvement can be realized through the following objectives:

- Consistent management interface – Consistent management practices and procedures will facilitate management across all applications and their underlying support structures. A consistent interface can simplify the management burden, leading to increased user efficiency.
- Reduced operation, administration and maintenance costs – Operation, administration and maintenance costs may be reduced through the availability of improved management products and increased standardization of the objects being managed.

Appendix B
Further Reading

This appendix contains some suggestions for further reading.

B.1 Business Scenarios

The Open Group has developed and published a number of business scenarios. They do not form part of the TOGAF documentation set and are made available in a separate section of The Open Group bookstore.[6] The current list of business scenarios follows:

Document Number	Title	Summary
K001	Directory-Enabled Enterprise	This Business Scenario explores the business and technical environment in which directories are deployed and analyzes the processes in which they are used. It also identifies the human and computing actors that participate in those processes, summarizes the requirements, and looks at the resulting technology architecture model.
K011	Directory in the Key Management Infrastructure	The goal of this Business Scenario is to identify the standards needed in commercial off-the-shelf directory products to realize the Key Management Infrastructure, to enable design and manufacture by product vendors and procurement by customers. While a key management infrastructure is needed for cryptographic technologies other than public key, this scenario concentrates on the key management infrastructures for PKI.

---

6 Refer to www.opengroup.org/bookstore/catalog.

Document Number	Title	Summary
K021	Executive on the Move	This Business Scenario investigates the problem of providing effective IT support to executives while they are away from their normal places of work, either at other locations, or in transit. It was developed by the Mobile and Directory Working Group of The Open Group in order to explore the requirements for Directories to support Mobile Computing and Communications.
K022	Interoperable Enterprise	This Business Scenario describes the problem caused by the lack of the right information to the right person at the right time (in technical terms, a lack of interoperability) preventing organizations from achieving their business objectives. This Business Scenario will be used as the basis for achieving agreement to the business issues, and to drive towards standards-based solutions that IT suppliers can deliver to their customers.
K023	Identity Management	This Business Scenario explores the requirements for identity management, the environment within which it must exist, and the implementation architectures that have been proposed for it.
K031	Certification	Certification impacts processes in standards development, product development, solutions, marketing, and management. The key questions are what, where, how, and when do you need certification. This document captures some crucial thoughts that require attention when considering certification. The Open Group is sponsoring a broad look at the certification area. This report documents the first step in that journey by documenting the thoughts of those that attended a Business Scenario Workshop to discuss the merits and pitfalls of certification.

Document Number	Title	Summary
K042	Measurement of Quality of Digital Information	This Business Scenario was developed by The Open Group in order to ascertain the requirements for measuring information quality. It explores the business and technical environment and processes, and the human and computer actors involved in information management. It identifies five important quality dimensions for measurement, and makes specific requirements for standardization of metadata, tagging, and metrics to enable enterprises to measure and improve their information quality.
K061	Identifiers in the Enterprise	This Business Scenario was developed by the Core Identifier Work Group, a joint initiative of The Open Group, the Network Applications Consortium (NAC), and the Distributed Management Task Force (DMTF) in order to develop an understanding of the requirements for core identifiers. This Business Scenario builds on an earlier draft Business Scenario developed by the Identity Management Work Area of The Open Group in order to ascertain the requirements for identity management products to support a standard representation of core identity.

B.2   TOGAF White Papers

The TOGAF White Papers comprise a body of knowledge about TOGAF contributed both by members and non-members of The Open Group Architecture Forum, for the benefit of TOGAF users world-wide.

They do not form part of the TOGAF documentation set, and in particular they are not approved by The Open Group formal adoption processes and do not represent the formal consensus of The Open Group

Architecture Forum. For that reason they are made available from an informational web site,[7] separate from the main TOGAF 8 documentation.

The current list of White Papers follows. The document number is the reference to obtain the document from The Open Group's online bookstore.

Title, Author(s), and Abstract
Service-Oriented Architecture (SOA) White Paper (Doc. No. W074) *By The Open Group SOA Working Group* This White Paper sets out the understanding that has been reached by the SOA Working Group of SOA and its relation to enterprise architecture, and in particular to TOGAF, in order to communicate that understanding to the rest of The Open Group and to the IT industry at large, and to provide a basis for the further development of the work program of the SOA Working Group.
TOGAF™ and COBIT® - Mapping of TOGAF 8.1 with COBIT 4.0 (Doc. No. W072) *By The IT Governance Institute® (ITGI®)* This document provides a detailed mapping of TOGAF 8.1 with COBIT 4.0 and also contains the classification of the standards discussed in this publication, as presented in the overview document COBIT Mapping: Overview of International IT Guidance, 2nd Edition. This mapping helps enterprise architects and auditors using the COBIT framework to consider the requirements and value-add of The Open Group Architecture Framework (TOGAF) 8.1, and *vice versa*. This White Paper is available as two parts in separate documents. Part I contains the actual TOGAF 8.1/COBIT 4.0 mapping. The research supporting the mapping is available in Part II (Doc. No. W072A) and consists of the following appendices: Appendix 1: Plan and Organize Appendix 2: Acquire and Implement Appendix 3: Deliver and Support Appendix 4: Monitor and Evaluate Appendix 5: Harmonization of Terms and Concepts

---

7 http://www.opengroup.org/architecture/wp/

Title, Author(s), and Abstract
TOGAF™ ADM/MDA® Synergy Project, Integration Proof-of-Concept Results (Doc. No. W073) *By Chris Armstrong, President, Armstrong Process Group, Inc., Judith Cerenzia, TEAMS Program Manager, Penn State University, Ed Harrington, Executive VP & COO, Model Driven Solutions, Pete Rivett, Chief Technology Officer, Adaptive, Inc., and Fred Waskiewicz, Director of Standards, Object Management Group* This White Paper discusses the role of Torpedo Enterprise Advanced Modeling and Simulation (TEAMS) in the TOGAF ADM/MDA Synergy Project, which is demonstrating the viability of using OMG specifications to describe Open Group standards. The Synergy Project first developed a formal process model, which laid the foundation for mapping ADM work products to elements of OMG specifications. TEAMS verified this mapping by formalizing an enterprise architecture, documenting business processes and requirements, and achieving a business-driven technology solution. The result demonstrates how the synergy of the TOGAF ADM/MDA technologies added value and enabled TEAMS to achieve their end product.
TOGAF™ and ITIL® (Doc. No. W071) *By Serge Thorn, Merck Serono International SA* This White Paper considers how the Information Technology Infrastructure Library (ITIL) and The Open Group Architecture Framework (TOGAF) can be used together, with a detailed comparison and mapping between the two.
TOGAF and the US Department of Defense Architecture Framework (DoDAF) (Doc. No. W061) *Developed by Terry Blevins (MITRE Corporation), Dr. Fatma Dandashi (MITRE Corporation), Judith Jones (Architecting-the-Enterprise Ltd.), and Rolf Siegers (Raytheon Company)* This document presents the results of an industry working group's analysis of the relationships between The Open Group Architecture Framework (TOGAF) and the US Department of Defense Architecture Framework (DoDAF). Complementary areas between the two are also identified.

Title, Author(s), and Abstract
Guide to Security Architecture in TOGAF ADM (Doc. No. W055) *By David Jackson, IBM and Michael Barrett, Johnson & Johnson* The goal of this White Paper is to explain what security considerations need to be addressed in the TOGAF ADM for the guidance of enterprise architects and system designers. Its primary purpose is as input to the Architecture Forum, for integrating security considerations into their development of the next version of TOGAF (designated TOGAF9). We also anticipate it will be of value to system architects and designers who include information security considerations in their designs.
TOGAF/MDA Mapping *By Pete Rivett, CTO, Adaptive Inc., John Spencer, Director, The Open Group Architecture Forum, and Fred Waskiewicz, OMG Director of Standards* This White Paper is one of a series of documents produced by a unique collaboration between three leading consortia in the IT industry: The Integration Consortium; OMG; and The Open Group. Building on an earlier White Paper published jointly by OMG and The Open Group, this White Paper provides a mapping between two sets of industry standards – the TOGAF Architecture Development Method (ADM) for Enterprise Architecture, developed by The Open Group Architecture Forum; and OMG's Model Driven Architecture® (MDA) family of modeling standards. The Integration Consortium intends to use this mapping as the basis of its own Global Integration Framework (GIF), and has performed the crucial role of user of the TOGAF/MDA mapping in this collaborative effort.

Title, Author(s), and Abstract

A Real Options Perspective to Enterprise Architecture as an Investment Activity

By Pallab Saha, Institute of Systems Science, National University of Singapore

The ever-increasing expenditure on information technology (IT) is accompanied by an increasing demand to measure the business value of the investment. This has prompted enterprises to take an architectural view of their information systems (IS) and supporting technologies. However, many crucial enterprise architecture frameworks and guidelines are characterized by lack of adequate theoretical or conceptual foundations. Important but inadequately formulated concepts include architectural assessments, governance, and architecture maturity models. These, though central to the enterprise architecture development process, remain in their current formulations largely wisdom-driven rather than engineering-based approaches. Absence of adequate scientific or mathematical foundations for enterprise design and engineering significantly impede enterprise architecture initiatives. The current body of knowledge is limited to reference architectures where the implementation challenges are left to the enterprises themselves.

This White Paper views enterprise architecture development as largely a process of decision-making under uncertainty and incomplete knowledge. Taking value maximization as the primary objective of the enterprise architecture decision-making process, the paper attempts to develop guidelines for value enhancement. The paper assumes that portion of the value of enterprise architecture initiative is in the form of embedded options (real options), which provide architects with valuable flexibility to change plans, as uncertainties are resolved over time. Plausibility of using such an approach to develop a better account of critical enterprise architecture practice is focused on three areas:

The timing of critical architectural decisions

Architecture development for adaptability and change

Phased approach to enterprise architecture maturity enhancement

Title, Author(s), and Abstract
Analyzing The Open Group Architecture Framework from the GERAM Perspective *By Pallab Saha, Institute of Systems Science, National University of Singapore* This White Paper analyzes The Open Group Architecture Framework (TOGAF) Enterprise Edition and its mapping onto the Generalized Enterprise Reference Architecture and Methodology (GERAM) framework/ISO IS 15704:2000 requirements. The analysis compares and contrasts these frameworks on multiple aspects that include: lifecycle phases, temporality and succession, modeling frameworks, modeling languages, methodologies, entity types, and reference models. The paper then discusses the role of TOGAF in the context of GERAM-compliant enterprise architecture development including suggestions for issues and areas to be addressed. Keywords: Enterprise Engineering, Enterprise Modeling, Technical Reference Model
TOGAF ADM and MDA® (Doc. No. W052) *By Terence J Blevins, The Open Group, John Spencer, The Open Group, and Fred Waskiewicz, OMG* In this White Paper The Object Management Group™ (OMG™) and The Open Group detail the synergies between The Open Group's TOGAF ADM and OMG's Model Driven Architecture® (MDA®), highlighting the benefits of using both methods to develop an architecture using the TOGAF ADM and then implement that architecture using MDA.
DSDM (Dynamic Systems Development Method) and TOGAF (The Open Group Architecture Framework) *A joint publication of the DSDM Consortium and The Open Group Architecture Forum* This paper aims to show that using a combination of the Dynamic Systems Development Method (DSDM) Framework and The Open Group Architecture Framework will help discover what architecture is currently in place, what architecture is needed that supports technology diversity and flexibility, and aid the projects defined for implementing the chosen architecture.

Glossary

ADM

Architecture Development Method

Architecture Framework

A tool for assisting in the prod=uction of architectures. An architecture framework consists of a Technical Reference Model, a method for architecture development, and a list of component standards, specifications, products, and their inter-relationships that can be used to build up architectures.

Architecture

Architecture has two meanings depending upon its contextual usage:
A formal description of a system, or a detailed plan of the system at component level to guide its implementation, or
The structure of components, their inter-relationships, and the principles and guidelines governing their design and evolution over time.

Architecture Continuum

A part of the Enterprise Continuum. The Architecture Continuum provides a repository of architecture elements with increasing detail and specialization. This Continuum begins with foundational definitions like reference models, core strategies, and basic building blocks. From there it spans to Industry Architectures and all the way to an organization's specific architecture.

Enterprise

The highest level in an organization; includes all missions and functions.

Enterprise Continuum

Comprises two complementary concepts: the Architecture Continuum and the Solutions Continuum. Together these are a range of definitions with increasing specificity, from foundational definitions and agreed enterprise strategies all the way to architectures and implementations in specific organizations. Such coexistence of abstraction and concreteness in an enterprise can be a real source of confusion. The Enterprise Continuum also doubles as a powerful tool to turn confusion and resulting conflicts into progress.

Information System

The computer-based portion of a business system.

Repository

A system that manages all of the data of an enterprise, including data and process models and other enterprise information. Hence, the data in a repository is much more extensive than that in a data dictionary, which generally defines only the data making up a database.

Solutions Continuum

A part of the Enterprise Continuum. The Solutions Continuum contains implementations of the corresponding definitions in the Architecture Continuum.

	In this way it becomes a repository of re-usable solutions for future implementation efforts.
Technical Reference Model	A structure which allows the components of an information system to be described in a consistent manner.
Time Horizon	The timeframe over which the potential impact is to be measured.
TRM	Technical Reference Model
View	A representation of a whole system from the perspective of a related set of concerns.
Viewpoint	A specification of the conventions for constructing and using a view. A viewpoint acts as a pattern or template of the view, from which to develop individual views. A viewpoint establishes the purposes and audience for a view, the ways in which the view is documented (e.g., for visual modeling), and the ways in which it is used (e.g., for analysis).

Index